Self-evaluation at the Celestial Mirror

Am I hosting Multiple Personalities?

A.C. Chandrahasan Johnson.MD

Self-evaluation at the Celestial Mirror

Am I hosting Multiple Personalities?

A.C. Chandrahasan Johnson

Assisted by

Satyabama Johnson

Edited by
Judah Vincent
Vasanth Appasamy

Copyright © 2012 by A.C. Chandrahasan Johnson. MD

Self-Evaluation At The Celestial Mirror
Am I Hosting Multiple Personalities?
by A.C. Chandrahasan Johnson. MD

Printed in the United States of America

ISBN 9781625092380

All rights reserved solely by the author. The author guarantees all contents are original and do not infringe upon the legal rights of any other person or work. No part of this book may be reproduced in any form without the permission of the author. The views expressed in this book are not necessarily those of the publisher.

Unless otherwise indicated, Bible quotations are taken from The New International Version, New Living Translation, and King James Version of the Bible

www.xulonpress.com

Foreword

*A*uthor of over a dozen books on themes such as salvation, peace, love and anger control, the eminent medical professional turned Christian writer Dr. A. C. Johnson this time takes a close look at "self". The title Self Evaluation at the Celestial Mirror which I have had the privilege of perusing a number of times in the course of editing, is a work that bids fair to lay bare all our inner most fears, suspicions, anxieties, concerns, prejudices and worries rather in the manner of an expert Psychiatrist. That it does so on the basis of the Word of God makes it possible to look for wholesome deliverance with the aid of the Holy Spirit.

Self Evaluation at the Celestial Mirror also contains a collection of nuggets of truth the Author labels syndromes. In this section, the Radiology expert that he is, Dr. Johnson is able to see through our personalities and expose the subtle games we play with our selves and others in our circle - all of them derived from Bible characters; a rare insight indeed !

Even a casual reading of the book is bound to ask questions of the reader as to why he does what he does and the editor certainly was not exempt from this intense scrutiny.

Let the beauty of Jesus be seen in us

Judah S. G. Vincent. B.E

"But if you are unwilling to obey the Lord, then decide today whom you will obey.................But as for me and my family, we will serve the Lord."

Joshua 24:15 (TLB)

Table of Contents

Part 1

Introduction 17
Types of Mirrors we use xxii

Part 2

A) How many "self's are there, hosted by
   each one of us the humanity?..37

B) Selective Biblical references in self-evaluation
   and where am I? 42

C) What are my God given gifts or talents, and where are
   they now? 68

Part 3

A) Am I salt of New Testament, or the pillar
   of salt of Old Testament? 89

B) What kind of Light am I? Flickering?
Smoke smothered? 98

Part 4

The Biblical Syndromes as the mirrors for, reflecting our own self errors

1 Aaron Syndrome 106
2 Abraham Syndrome 108
3 Absalom Syndrome 109
4 Adam Syndrome..111
5 Amnon Syndrome 113
6 Ananias & Sapphire Syndrome 115
7 Athaliah Syndrome...116
8 Caiaphas Syndrome 117
9 Cain Syndrome..118
10 Korah Dathan(KD) Syndrome 119
11 Demas Syndrome 120
12 Diatrephes Syndrome 121
13 Eli Syndrome 122
14 Elijah Syndrome..123
15 Elisha Syndrome 125
16 Esau Syndrome 126
17 Eve Syndrome 127
18 Felix Syndrome 128
19 Gehazi Syndrome...129
20 Haman Syndrome...130
21 Hananiah Syndrome 132
22 Herod Syndrome 133
23 Herodias Syndrome 135
24 Hezekiah Syndrome 136
25 Isaac Syndrome 138
26 Jezebel Syndrome 139
27 Jacob Syndrome 141

Table Of Contents

28 Job's friends' Syndrome 142
29 Jonah Syndrome 143
30 Jonadab Syndrome 144
31 Joseph Syndrome 145
32 Judas Iscariot Syndrome 146
33 King David Syndrome 147
34 Laban Syndrome 149
35 Laodicea Church Syndrome 149
36 Lot Syndrome 150
37 Lying Prophet Syndrome 154
38 Martha Syndrome 156
39 Mordecai Syndrome 157
40 Nicodemus Syndrome 158
41 Pharaoh Syndrome 159
42 Pharisee Syndrome 161
43 Pilate Syndrome 162
44 Prodigal son Syndrome 163
45 Rebecca Syndrome 165
46 Sadusee Syndrome 167
47 Samson Syndrome 169
48 Saul Syndrome 170
49 Scribe Syndrome 171
50 Shimeii Syndrome 172
51 Simon the Sorcerer Syndrome 173
52 Solomon Syndrome 174
53 Son in House Syndrome 176
54 Thyatira Church Syndrome 177
55 The Gullible Prophet of Judah Syndrome 179

Part 5

Self-based Behavioral Problems,
and conflicts in Homes and therapies 185

Reference 201

Acknowledgements 203

List of Phobias from Wikipedia 205

PART 1

Introduction

Before taking up any study or vocation, we need to make sure that we will not regret our decision nor get burnt up. When we take up a work that we really like, we are 'paid' to enjoy our lives. We cannot like a job or specialty, just because someone we like has something similar or recommends it. We need to know what makes us tick, and what ticks us off! When we know ourselves better, we can function better; we can then discard things that are harmful to us. That means we need to know a little bit about our "self"

> Let us honestly assess ourselves
>
> Lest we make asses of ourselves

The people of Gadarenes may or may not have known the name of the fearful man from the tombs in the hills, who terrorized them worse than a tyrant legionnaire. When the Lord Jesus confronted him and asked him for his name, he answered that it was 'legion', because he had many spirits living within him. The insane man had lost his original identity, and took on the identity of the evil spirits within him - until Jesus healed him, and gave him a new identity. A new identity of a responsible missionary was given to him. The people who had owned the secret forbidden "swine-herd" treasure did not want Jesus to stay with them any longer, for they had "swine on their mind"! The healed man however wanted to go with Jesus. Nevertheless, Jesus advised him to stay with the people of Gadarenes, so that he will bring a blessing to the local people and get the swine off their minds. By the time Jesus went to the other side of Galilee by boat, the people had changed by reason of witnessing by the "ex-legion missionary". The people, who once rejected Jesus, now gathered in crowds and flocked to meet Jesus and to receive healing from Him. The woman with chronic bleeding from the uterus was healed when she touched the hem of His garment. The Gadarenes were also privileged to witness the daughter of the ruler of their synagogue raised from dead by Jesus.

As a student of medicine, I postulate that the swineherd had serious parasites infection called Cysticercus, a tapeworm that affects humans who eat pork. The worms affect many parts of the human body, including the brain. There was no remedy for this fatal disease. Jesus with His divine perception mercifully protected the lives of the people by permitting demise of the sick swine, even though the local people were not aware of the danger. The Lord Jesus never left a loss behind Him. He only left blessings behind by His actions. He would not have allowed the loss of people's property. Please read Mark 5 chapter and meditate on it. You will understand how the man living among the remains of the dead became the salvaging hero of Gadarenes because of the confrontation of his self with Jesus. This opportunity is available for every one of us.

We must not compare ourselves with any other human being, whether good or bad, for it can result in making excuses for our own blemishes. If we compare ourselves with someone we consider inferior, we are liable to become proud and end up self-satisfied. On the other hand, if we compare ourselves with someone we think is superior, we become discouraged and envious. The Bible advises against comparing ourselves with (the faulty) ourselves.

2 Corinthians 10:12 (TLB): Oh, don't worry, I wouldn't dare say that I am as wonderful as these other men who tell you how good they are! Their trouble is that they are only comparing themselves with each other and measuring themselves against their own little ideas. What stupidity!

Introduction

Self-examination:

The reason why we need to go to our mirror frequently is to check not only our faces, but also to seek God to heal us. The memory of our outer man from the mirror is brief and fleeting. James 1:23-24 (KJV): For if any be a hearer of the word, and not a doer, he is like unto a man beholding his natural face in a glass. For he beholdeth himself, and goeth his way, and straightway forgetteth what manner of man he was". Let us keep the Mirror provided by God (His Word) in our hearts and minds always. Hebrews 10:16 (KJV): This is the covenant that I will make with them after those days, saith the Lord. I will put my laws into their hearts, and in their minds will I write them.

Caution:

Self-evaluation presented in this book is for curative purpose, not for superficial touch ups and masking blemishes with paints or coatings. Therefore, it cannot be a "do it yourself" method. It calls for integrity and honesty. Self-confrontation will bring up stark memories of our dark past and convict us of moral failures. Though we justify ourselves and make excuses, complications follow.

The self-evaluation must bring us to the Cross of Jesus, who will connect us to the Mercy Seat of God. Otherwise, our confrontation of our past and present sins will bring guilt and condemnation upon us. Condemnation is devoid of hope. Loss of hope will drive us into despair, depression and deep melancholy - why even suicide! If on the other-hand, when self-evaluation is at the Cross, the Spirit of God brings to us conviction of our sins past and present, and makes us aware that it is our sins that caused Jesus to be punished in our place. The Holy Spirit enables us to repent and confess our sins to God. The love of Jesus, who, while even when upon the Cross for our sins prayed "Father forgive them for they know not what they do", will forgive us, cleanse us, and give us a new heart to host Him and the Holy Spirit eternally. Our subsequent daily self-evaluation (like going to the mirror in the bathroom for facial clean up) will keep us connected with God to enable even our appearances to become the reflection of God, for the benefit of all who come across our path.

- **The Bible encourages examining ourselves**

Lamentations 3:40 (NASB): Let us examine and probe our ways, and let us return to the LORD

1 Corinthians 11:31 (KJV): For if we would judge ourselves, we should not be judged.

    Whether we believe or not, there is judgment after we die. We - each one of us - will have to answer to God (from whom nothing is hid) for our every thought, word and action. Our voluntary self-confrontation at Calvary will provide us an advocate who paid for our pardon, so that He can be our shield on the day of God's judgment.
    Self-confrontation does not and must not make us into judges. Only God is the judge.
    Self-confrontation must take us to Jesus, who is the healer, forgiver and our advocate during the final judgment.

1 John 2:3-6 (TLB): 3 And how can we be sure that we belong to him? By looking within ourselves: are we really trying to do what he wants us to? 4 Someone may say, "I am a Christian; I am on my way to heaven; I belong to Christ." But if he doesn't do what Christ tells him to, he is a liar.5 But those who do what Christ tells them to will learn to love God more and more. That is the way to know whether or not you are a Christian.6 Anyone who says he is a Christian should live as Christ did.

1 Thessalonians 5:21 (NASB77): But examine everything carefully; hold fast to that which is good.

- There is a great need to carry out self-examination to prevent us getting perverted.

Introduction

2 Corinthians 13:5 (KJV): Examine yourselves, whether ye be in the faith; prove your own selves. Know ye not your own selves, how that Jesus Christ is in you, except ye be reprobates?

- Self-evaluation brings into us good sense and responsibility

2 Kings 7:3-4 (KJV): 3 And there were four leprous men at the entering in of the gate: and they said one to another, "Why sit we here until we die? 4 If we say, "We will enter into the city, then the famine is in the city, and we shall die there: and if we sit still here, we die also. Now therefore come, and let us fall unto the host of the Syrians: if they save us alive, we shall live; and if they kill us, we shall but die."

- Self-examination will help us to return to the Lord

Lamentations 3:40 (NASB): Let us examine and probe our ways, and let us return to the LORD.

- Self-examination is recommended before taking the Lord's Supper.

1 Corinthians 11:28-29 (TLB): 28 That is why a man should examine himself carefully before eating the bread and drinking from the cup. 29 For if he eats the bread and drinks from the cup unworthily, not thinking about the body of Christ and what it means, he is eating and drinking God's judgment upon himself; for he is trifling with the death of Christ.

- Self-examination is a stepping-stone for us to be transformed to His likeness

Romans 12:2 (NASB): And do not be conformed to this world, but be transformed by the renewing of your mind, so that you may prove what the will of God is, that which is good and acceptable and perfect.

- Self-estimation demands honesty and no excuses or justifications

Romans 12:3 (TLB): As God's messenger I give each of you God's warning: Be honest in your estimate of yourselves, measuring your value by how much faith God has given you.

- Self-evaluation will show if we really love God or just say that we do.

1 John 2: 9-10: Examine your selves to see if you have love for others. This is the main index of loving God. If we do not love others in thought, word and deed, we do not love God.

- Self-evaluation can restore relationship with God the Father, through Jesus

Luke 15:21 (KJV): And the son said unto him, Father, I have sinned against heaven, and in thy sight, and am no more worthy to be called thy son.

Lamentations 3:40 (NIV): Let us examine our ways and test them, and let us return to the LORD.

Joel 2:13 (KJV): And rend your heart, and not your garments, and turn unto the LORD your God: for he is gracious and merciful, slow to anger, and of great kindness, and repenteth him of the evil.

Matthew 7:5 (NIV): You hypocrite, first take the plank out of your own eye, and then you will see clearly to remove the speck from your brother's eye.

2 Corinthians 13:5 (NIV): Examine yourselves to see whether you are in the faith; test yourselves. Do you not realize that Christ Jesus is in you—unless, of course, you fail the test?

Some people want to give up physical comforts, their money, and even their possessions to ease their conscience of guilt, and some seek after fame and name. Nobel Prize is not a noble gesture, but an effort to assuage and numb the guilty conscience of the creators of the explosive device - dynamite.

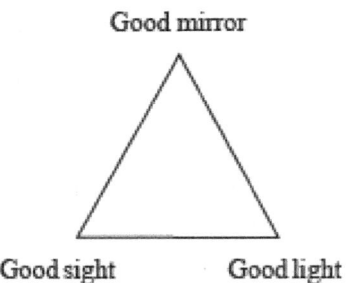

We use three types of mirror in our day to day lives:

1) Plane mirror
2) Convex mirror
3) Concave mirror

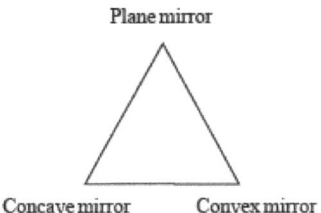

The plane mirror reflects the object in front. However, it reverses positions - right to left and vice versa.

Convex mirror will magnify the object in front, provided the object is within the focal point of convexity. This is used for close shaving, and removing black heads or blemishes from our faces.

Concave mirror will minify the object; it is used in cars and buses as rear view mirror.

These three mirrors will provide information only superficially, on the surface. They are good for surface blemish detection, not for underlying defects for which we need other devices that can see through our bodies. X-Rays, Ultra-sound units and Magnetic Imaging devices act as mirrors to show the inside of our bodies. However it is only the Bible which can show the blemishes inside our minds and souls. The Bible shows the blemishes in our thoughts, the different personalities within us producing conflicts and the deep emotional turmoil within us. The Bible can not only reveal them to us, but can also help in cleaning and curing them.

When we carry out self-examination, the plane mirror is what we need to use, taking into consideration the apparent reversal of right and the left. To emphasize the importance of this phenomenon, let me narrate a humorous incident. I was in the process of getting recognition for an international accreditation for teaching a technology program in our Radiology department, at the Christian Medical College at Vellore, South India. It needed the personal inspection, approval and authorization of the administrator from UK for collaboration. I had been in touch with that person when I was doing my Radiology Fellowship (FFR) in London. After I returned to India and had the department ready for approval, I invited the Administrator to our hospital in India. That person wanted to eat authentic South Indian food at my home, came to our house, rejected the cutlery and insisted on eating with fingers just as a South Indian like me would. After the lunch was over, my guest challenged me to find any fault in the gastronomic performance. I said everything was perfect except that while sitting across me and trying to imitate me, the guest used the left hand to eat with, instead of the right, which I used. I explained the understanding and applications for the right hand and the left in the local culture. That person was very embarrassed by the "mirror-imaging" mistake, and could not find any objection to approving our department for the Technology program to be accepted for UK collaboration! However, I need to emphasize that the standard of our department was far higher than their requirement, and did not need any gastric bribery or 'sly persuasions' for approval!

There are trick mirrors to make a fat person look thin, a skinny person look hefty, or the short one to look towering and tall. They are at best 'lie-ing' mirrors used for entertainment only. If, we resort to using trick mirrors, the trick mirrors make truth appear as lie, lie as truth; white as black, black as white; light as dark and darkness as light!

Trick mirrors

It is wrong and unacceptable, and it resembles the use of the current culture of 'politically correct views and language' upon truth and morality. That is the reason we need to be brutally honest in self-evaluation. The modern trick mirrors offer the possibility of accepting pollution and perversion as alternate ways of living so prevalent today, and yet maintain our 'so called' self-esteem. This concept allows us to love ourselves and forgive ourselves as we continue to live the way we do, regardless of the moral health of our home and future generations! If God does not forgive a person, any amount of forgiving oneself or approving oneself is worthless and meaningless.

There are three important factors that loom when we apply self-examination.

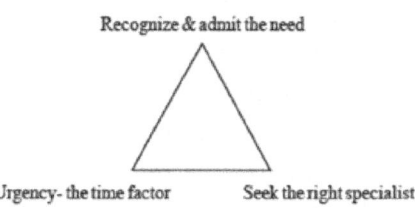

1) The first is to recognize honestly whether there is any problem that needs to be identified. If we think that there is no problem, we may be ignoring or denying existing problems.

It is then that we will likely fall into a trap called 'self-deception'.
2) The second is to seriously consider the urgency of the problems which need to be dealt with. We must know whether we have to deal with the problem detected at once or with-in minutes, or hours, or whether we can put it off safely for a few days.
3) The third is to know where to go for help, and to whom

We will never learn what is wrong with us unless we are willing to seek the right specialist. In this age of information super-highways, we have to be careful to filter out the garbage and go to the specialist who is qualified and experienced, with a record of successful treatment. When we go to the specialist, the 'healer' of our sickness, we need to be honest and transparent, and not withhold anything needed for the remedy. If we hide vital information from the healer, we will suffer by lying to the physician in this life; and we will lose all hope of eternal life in the next, by avoiding God.

It takes knowledge to diagnose or identify, as well as to apply the right treatment at the appropriate time. Only a few things can be done through self-help (not the same as self-confrontation). All chronic, concealed or complicated problems need the help of a qualified, experienced, compassionate and capable specialist. In such matters, our appointment alone is insufficient. It requires our compliance, application, and obedience to the specialist's instructions, during not only the process of diagnosis, but also the treatment, and the follow-ups. In my past, I have come across numerous patients who decided to modify the treatment prescribed and got into trouble. When medicines were 'given' for one week, the patients decided that if they took it all in one day, they would get better sooner! Most medicines have mild or severe side-reactions. When patients suffer, and become aware of the side reactions, they stop taking the medicine, blaming the medicine or the physician; or even modify the recommendations without consulting the physician. Even well educated people are not exempt from these tendencies!

Types Of Mirrors We Use

The information provided in this small book is applicable to all the human residents of the planet earth, whatever their religion, color, creed, age, sex or nationality.

Accessories needed for self-evaluation:

As mentioned earlier, we need good light to illuminate our faces and our bodies, in order to see our reflection in the mirror. We also need good eyesight to recognize what we see as our 'reflection'. If our eyesight is not good, we need increased acuity of other sensations. Increased hearing will help to listen to, understand and obey the physician's (or God's) instructions. Increase in tactile (touch) sensations enables blind people to feel the healer's (or God's) guiding hands, to read in Braille the prescriptions and advice.

We go to physicians periodically to find out if we are in good health, or, if we have some trouble with any part of our body underlying the skin, hidden deep within us. The physicians also need different kinds of mirrors, which we can call as "lights" and different kinds of tools in order to evaluate different organs of the body. Samples of our excretions, secretions, and blood are drawn which will also offer important information about our health with the use of microscopes, spectroscopes etc.

There are people who do not want to know, even when there is serious sickness within them. Most of such people are cowards, and some others are fatalists, who have lost 'hope'. Some others wishfully want to think positively, rejecting or refusing to say, or admit to anything 'negative'. They hope that by doing so, the problems will disappear. Such people suffer 'denial and self-deception' due to a false sense of 'self-justification'. I have seen numerous patients who refused treatment of cancers, when the cancers presented as painless lumps (tumors) and were easily treatable or removable. Sadly, they returned when the tumors had advanced, and became painful, foul smelling, ulcerated, fungating, with multiple secondaries.

However, there are some religious groups, who believe that healing should only be a divine intervention as a miracle, and that medical intervention implies a lack of faith in God. An extreme end of such fanatics is seen in a group who handle venomous snakes in their religious frenzy. Those who die by snake bite are supposed to have little or no faith!!

Is it better to do self-confrontation, or take it to another person who is a counselor, or therapist? Self-evaluation is not expensive. Physicians and counselors are very expensive and undependable. No human being will be completely honest in exposing himself or herself to another human. Self-confrontation using the Bible as God's offer of "mirror, light, and vision" is found to be very dependable by millions of people. For, this brings us to the Cross, where Jesus took the punishment due for you and me. It is at the Cross where the convicting Holy Spirit reveals our hidden sins and errors to us, and enables honest heartfelt (contrite) repentant confessions to our all-knowing Creator. Please note that our repentant confession will be mere lip service when not followed by necessary corrections, willingness to change, and restitutions when we receive Jesus. It is then the light of God comes within us, the power and grace of God operate in our souls and our spirits as both diagnostic and therapeutic healing force, connecting us to God and to life eternal.

The Mirrors we need also act as our Compass (direction for our lives). Three groups of people use the mirrors more often than others:

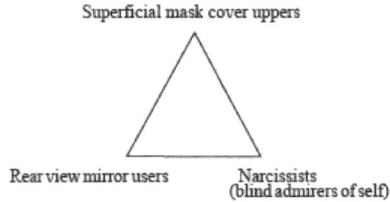

1) The first group is 'glued' to the mirror, preening repeatedly. This group is 'focused' on its own 'self' due to 'self-preoccupation' and not for self-evaluation. This group covers-up flaws with masking make-ups. They become hypocrites. Such people do not care to be good, but only want to look good for others who see them. Many patients with contagious diseases have done this in the past, not only allowing their own disease to advance unchecked, but also exposing others to their infections.

2) The second group with self-preoccupation may be allowing pride to ride and rule them, with self- indulgence, turning them into Narcissists. They think that they look better than others do, and are very pleased with themselves. Jesus compared them to whitewashed sepulchers.
3) The third group is like the reckless car drivers who drive forward fast without looking forward, only looking back into the rear view mirror. They gloat over people or other drivers they have overtaken, not realizing that they are heading towards danger while looking back. Or, they are also people who live in their past, remembering their sins and guilt, suppressed anger, and hurts. There-by they invite bitterness, self-pity, or loss of hope, driving 'them-selves' into depression or 'self-condemnation'. Their basic problem is an inflated and bloated Self. This is the main reason that our 'self' called the 'ego' should go out, and Christ should come in instead, whenever we attempt self- confrontation.

Self-confrontation will be useful, effective and powerful only after each individual's personal confrontation, and connection with Jesus the Savior. Self-confrontation does not imply self-help. We need to know where to obtain the best help for healing. We must remember that Jesus came as a substitute sacrifice for our sins and to pay the penalty in our stead. Are we willing to receive Him into our lives? Jesus removed all the barriers (intermediaries) to enable us come to God personally, through His own shed blood at the Cross. This is good news.

God offers us two major blessings through Jesus.

1) One is mercy, meaning that we need His merciful forgiveness for our sins of commission and sins of omission, which deserve severe eternal punishment.
2) The second is grace, meaning we are 'offered' something, which we do not deserve, nor can earn by our best efforts. That is the 'free gift of Salvation', an offer of eternal adoption as God's children. Jesus took upon Himself the punishment meant for us, each one of us. If the offer is not ac-

cepted, the human one to whom it is offered, rejects it. The consequences are eternal! Jesus is eternal life. To get connected with Him means we are with God eternally.

While looking at the mirror for self-evaluation, as the good Book says, if we compare ourselves with ourselves, we will go very wrong. For, we the humans are depraved and flawed, even to hosting serious perversions, driving us to self-destruction and suicide.

2 Corinthians 10:12 (NIV): We do not dare to classify or compare ourselves with some who commend themselves. When they measure themselves by themselves and compare themselves with themselves, they are not wise. We need to have an honest, tested, universal 'yard-stick', a 'gold standard', or 'mirror' for correct evaluation and measurement. This reliable 'mirror', is Jesus and His teachings in the New Testament.

The teachings of Jesus are the only yardstick applicable universally, whatever be the religion, race, or region. For, Jesus did not bring another religion, but a relationship offering a LOVING, GENTLE, PEACEFUL WAY OF LIFE for us to have,

1) Love for all, however undeserving,
2) Peace with all, despite injustice, or persecutions.
3) Consideration of others above 'self', and to serve others.

No religion can offer it; only the person of Jesus makes it possible through the way of the Cross.

When you look at yourself in a Mirror, it can lead you to

Is there anyone in this age that does not go to a mirror more than once a day? Does one not go back repeatedly to the mirror even on the same day?

> Mirror, mirror on the wall
>
> Show my errors big or small

Who needs self-confrontation/evaluation? If your answer is yes for any of the following, you need self-evaluation:

Do you get hurt when people ignore you, ignore your recommendations, talk badly behind you unjustly, cheat you, lie to you, lie about you or ill-treat you? If yes, it is your self-esteem which is hurting. Therefore, your 'Self' needs confrontation.

Are you shy, introverted, sensitive, avoid controversy and conflicts? If yes, your Self is too cautious and suffers self- inadequacy, and needs to be evaluated and set right.

Are you extroverted, bold, and confident with goals for your life? You have 'self and ego' that dominates you and you need to do self-evaluation to submit your real inside.

Are you carefree or extravagant with money, in order to enjoy what life has to offer? You need to do self-evaluation, as your Self is only interested in self-indulgence, spiritually a dangerous position.

Are you very careful with money, cut off any extravagance, almost miserly, carefully watching the bank balance, and the stock market? You need to do self-evaluation as your Self is suffering severe Insecurity, and is in need of real eternal security.

Are you self-effacing and timid? Your Self-controls you and draws you into a shell. You need to do self-evaluation at the Cross-to make you into a soldier of the Cross.

Are you anxious, and fearful and prone to worrying? Fear and faith cannot co-exist. Fear of God is a faith called reverence. Any other Fear is part of reliance upon self, and needs to be taken to the Cross and replaced with hope and trust in Almighty God.

Are you a person who gets irritated, and angry? It means that you have a hostile nature that will lead you into becoming bitter. The Bible warns us against the gall of bitterness.

Are you laid back, lazy and prone to procrastination and slothfulness? You have a problem of self-centeredness and self-indulgence, and need self-evaluation.

The following groups also need to do self-evaluation:

Fathers: - They are expected to have the loving forgiving heart of God the Father. Fathers need to protect and provide for the family, with a self-sacrificing nature. They are not to behave like the male animal lion, which depends on the females to provide and have the lion's share while the rest of the family waits until the gluttonous male moves away to sleep.

Mothers: - Mothers are to be embodiment of self-sacrifice for the family. If not, they will sadly "s'mother' the very dignity of womanhood.

Siblings: - Lest we like Cain murder our brother or cheat him like Jacob !

Family members and Friends:- When the God of peace, and the peace of God does not dwell in us, we will break peace to pieces.

Pastors and various clergy:- Churches are a collection of worshippers to function as members of the body of the Lord Jesus, who is the head of the church. Pastors are to guide the church members into nourishing pasture given in the word of God. The clergy must fully understand that the sheep (church members) belong to the Good Shepherd, and not to the employed (hireling) clergy.

Each Christian is like a blood cell: white, red or platelet. The churches are only parts of the body like the arms, legs, eyes, nose or mouth. The blood cells belong to the body of God. The blood must not be 'trapped' within one part of the body (church). The cells need

to go to the heart, then the lungs, get cleaned up and be empowered to go wherever the heart sends them. Many churches have a locally fatal condition called the Ainhum's disease, where a part of the body –usually a toe, develops a fibrous band around it, isolating itself and eventually cutting itself off, finally falling dead. Many preachers and pastors fall into the danger of trapping Christians as their 'sheepish flock' within their own 'impervious fences', and enforcing their doctrines upon them. They could eventually become a cultish group headed for total destruction, like Jim Jones' flock.
Preachers and Teachers:- Do you practice what you preach? Are you out of reach of what you preach or teach? Are you out of range of 'obeying' God's message through you, or even your own advice?

Do you pass on the pure 'message' of the Bible, or resort to your own 'massage'? Do you preach or teach what you believe and do, or are you hypocritical? Is your teaching for the good of the hearers and the society, or for your power and the purse? Your teaching must bring peace and good will, not create terrorists, psychopaths or social enemies.

Students: - So that they may study this book and apply it in their lives.

Health care workers:- Who need compassion for patient and not passion for their wallets.

Legal and the judiciary: - Who will also be judged in their turn

Politicians: - Who influence and even control the public for better or for worse.

Media workers: - The printed, audio and video media have a great potential for educating, for uplifting individuals, as well as the entire nation. They have the ability to brainwash or brain warp their audience acting as open gutters carrying the filth of their nation to every home and even flooding other nations. This will have the effect of a Pandemic epidemic.

Law enforcement workers:- So that they do not become outlaws to God

Soldiers: - So that they will know who the real enemies are.

Educational workers: - So that they may understand the difference between book information and the wisdom from above.

Rulers of nations:- To realize that they too will decay, get diseases, die and rot as any beggar on the street, or animals, birds, reptiles and fishes.

In fact, all of us human beings need to have periodic self-evaluation and apply necessary treatments. For every one of us will find many selves lurking within, causing hurt and harm. In short, everyone needs to do 'self-evaluation'.

PART 2

A) How many "selves" are there in each one of us?

The Bible calls 'self' as 'the flesh', which is a part of our inner man. There are numerous "selves" hosted by each one of us. Air hostesses have come to realize that the Indians are the smartest travelers. The hostesses have learned that they should offer fruit juice with "no ice" to Indian passengers. The other travelers get their glass or paper cup filled with ice and a couple of cubic centimeters of juice, which fills the cups to the brim. They are oblivious to the fact that they are really short changed as they sip the diluted drops of juice; their habit of wanting their drinks hard, warming on the ice rocks! When there are too many "selves" within us, there can only be a few drops of blessings, to quench our thirst for eternal life.

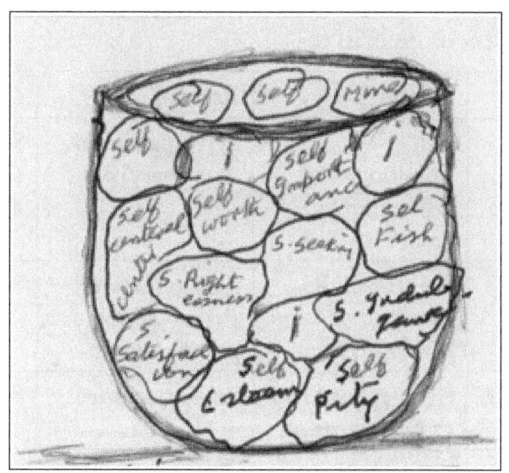

There are many types of "selves" within us, which influence and control us. Only a few of these are shown in the diagram. These worthless harmful pebbles of 'self" fill us to the brim and we cannot use the container (us) for getting the life giving Living water, or the bread of life which God offers. We can identify four groups of "selves". Some of them are godly, some good, some bad, and other ugly, using even our own moral standards. However, any self, even the best of its kind is a handicap. We need to get rid of all the "selves", and it is possible only when we are willing for our 'flesh' to be crucified. The term "flesh" here denotes non-matter 'desires and deep emotions'. Our body is part of our outer man, made of matter.

The bad and ugly "selves" need to be repented for, confessed, get forgiven and get rid-off along with grudges and guilt when a person first comes to the Cross.

The godly and good "selves" need to be removed from us to enable us to be used by God effectively. The godly and good "selves" in us cause us to behave like little immature children who try to help the mother in her kitchen or the father in the theatre (while he, a surgeon is performing a delicate operation) and end up by being a nuisance and a hindrance! For it would then be "WE, Our Selves" who are trying to help God to fulfill His purpose. Our selves, even with good intentions cause havoc among people and do not help God's purpose. We will discuss these later.

The four groups of Self are:-

Godly self	*Good self*	*Bad self*	*Ugly self*
Self-less *Self is crucified*	**Self-abandonment** *Giving up to God*	**Self-appointed** *No input from God*	**Self-indulgence** *Gives indigestion & belly-aching*
Self-sacrifice *At God's altar*	**Self-discipline** *Learn to become disciplined*	**Self-assertive** *Promoted by psychologists*	**Self-abuse**
Self-denial *Like Jesus did*	**Self-reliant** *Not to be a parasite*	**Self-assurance**	**Self-condemnation**

A) How Many "Selves" Are There In Each One Of Us?

Self-control *One of the Fruit of the Spirit*	Self-analysis	Self-consciousness	Self-delusion
Self-abnegation *With deep humility*	Self-awareness	Self-contradictory	Self-destructive
Self-Evaluation in-depth *At the Cross*	Self-concept *Not to think too highly*	Self-gratification	Self-hypnosis
Self-Confrontation *After reading this book*	Self-critical *To see through the Word -Bible*	Self-hatred	Self-immolation *suicide*
	Self-defense *Not to lose control*	Self-identity	Self-importance *Arrogant & asinine*
	Self-determination *To have a purpose*	Self-image	Self-justifying *Bad accountability*
	Self-discovery *At the Cross*	Self-incrimination	Self-mortification
	Self-disgust *When beholding Jesus on the Cross*	Self-induced	Self-mutilation *Self-penance is useless; only hurts us*
	Self-effacing *When repenting*	Self-inflicted	Self-exaltation *Arrogant*
	Self-made *With God's help*	Self-limited	Self-seeking *Self-centered*
	Self-motivated *To follow Jesus*	**Self-medication**	**Self-serving** *Self-centered*
	Self-preservation *Built into us*	Self-respect	Self-deception

39

	Self-realization *At the Cross*	**Self-satisfaction**	**Self-absorbed** *Self-centered*
	Self-perception	**Self-sufficient**	**Selfishness** *Self-centered*
	Self- restraint	**Self-ambition**	**Self – centered** *God needs to be in the center*
	Self -help	**Self-confidence**	**Self-righteousness** *White washed tombs*
	Self-acceptance	**Self-actualization**	**Self- worship** *Narcissism*
	Self-expression	**Self –esteem** *Promoted by psychologists, Pastors*	**Self- pity** *No pity on others self-centered*
		Self-denigration	**Self-willed**
		Self -promotion	**Sell-fish-ness** *We will stink even to Heaven*
	Self-Identity	**Self-seeking**	
		Self-worth *Promoted by psychologists*	**Self – importance** *Promoted by psychologists*

A) How Many "Selves" Are There In Each One Of Us?

		Self-forgiving *Promoted by psychologists, Pastors*	

B) Selective biblical reference in self-evaluation

– where am I?

*L*et us see what the Bible has to say about the various good, bad and the ugly selves in us.

The UGLY self

- Self-indulgence

Timothy 3:2 (NIV) People will be lovers of themselves, lovers of money, boastful, proud, abusive, disobedient to their parents, ungrateful, unholy

- Self-deception

James 1:22 (KJV) But be ye doers of the word, and not hearers only, deceiving your own selves.

- Self-importance

1 Samuel 16:7 (NIV) But the Lord said to Samuel, "Do not consider his appearance or his height, for I have rejected him. The Lord does not look at the things man looks at. Man looks at the outward appearance, but the Lord looks at the heart."

B) Selective Biblical Reference In Self-Evaluation

- Self-condemnation

1 John 3:20 (KJV) For if our heart condemn us, God is greater than our heart, and knoweth all things.

- Self-destructive

Mark 5:4 (NIV) For he had often been chained hand and foot, but he tore the chains apart and broke the irons on his feet. No one was strong enough to subdue him.

- Selfishness

2 Timothy 3:2 (NIV) People will be lovers of themselves, lovers of money, boastful, proud, abusive, disobedient to their parents, ungrateful, unholy, 1 Corinthians 10:24 (NIV) Nobody should seek his own good, but the good of others.

- Self-righteousness (is abomination to God)

Romans 10:3 (KJV) For they being ignorant of God's righteousness, and going about to establish their own righteousness, have not submitted themselves unto the righteousness of God.

Proverbs 30:12 (KJV) There is a generation that are pure in their own eyes, and yet is not washed from their filthiness.

Deuteronomy 9:4 (KJV) Speak not thou in thine heart, after that the LORD thy God hath cast them out from before thee, saying, For my righteousness the LORD hath brought me in to possess this land: but for the wickedness of these nations the LORD doth drive them out from before thee.

Matthew 23:25 (KJV)
Woe unto you, scribes and Pharisees, hypocrites! for ye make clean the outside of the cup and of the platter, but within they are full of extortion and excess.

Luke 18:11 (KJV) The Pharisee stood and prayed thus with himself, God, I thank thee, that I am not as other men are, extortioners, unjust, adulterers, or even as this publican.

- Self-righteousness is due to pride

2 Chronicles 26:16 (NIV) But after Uzziah became powerful, his pride led to his downfall. He was unfaithful to the LORD his God, and entered the temple of the LORD to burn incense on the altar of incense.

Instead of standing at the outskirts, beating on the breast and repenting saying 'God be merciful to me a sinner', some of us try to hide our wickedness. We cover up by putting on a holy show when we are corrupt. Pride in this case consorts with lies. Trying to fool others, we make fools of ourselves.

- Self-immolation/ Self-destruction

Matthew 27:5 (NIV) So Judas threw the money into the temple and left. Then he went away and hanged himself.

- Hypocrites need Self-confrontation, for they suffer Self-deception

Matthew 7:5 (NASB) You hypocrite, first take the log out of your own eye, and then you will see clearly to take the speck out of your brother's eye.

- False evaluation of self, dangers of false mirror images

2 Corinthians 10:12 (TLB) Oh, don't worry, I wouldn't dare say that I am as wonderful as these other men who tell you how good they are! Their trouble is that they are only comparing themselves with each other and measuring themselves against their own little ideas. What stupidity!

B) Selective Biblical Reference In Self-Evaluation

- Recognition seeking

Matthew 6:16-17 (TLB) And now about fasting. When you fast, declining your food for a spiritual purpose, don't do it publicly, as the hypocrites do, who try to look wan and disheveled so people will feel sorry for them. Truly, that is the only reward they will ever get.

- Self-delusion

Matthew 24:48 (NASB) But if that evil slave says in his heart, 'My master is not coming for a long time,'

Proverbs 14:12 (KJV) There is a way which seemeth right unto a man, but the end thereof are the ways of death.

- Self-exaltation

Isaiah 14:12-14 (KJV) 12 How art thou fallen from heaven, O Lucifer, son of the morning! how art thou cut down to the ground, which didst weaken the nations!13 For thou hast said in thine heart, I will ascend into heaven, I will exalt my throne above the stars of God: I will sit also upon the mount of the congregation, in the sides of the north: 14 I will ascend above the heights of the clouds; I will be like the most High.

Psalms 73:8-9 (NIV) 8 They scoff, and speak with malice; in their arrogance they threaten oppression. 9 Their mouths lay claim to heaven, and their tongues take possession of the earth.

Proverbs 16:18 (KJV) Pride goeth before destruction, and an haughty spirit before a fall.

- Self-elevation (Who is the greatest?)

Mark 9:33-35 (NASB) 33 They came to Capernaum; and when He was in the house, He began to question them, "What were you discussing on the way?" 34 But they kept silent, for on the way they had discussed with one another which of them was the greatest. 35 Sitting down, He called the twelve and said to them, "If anyone wants to be first, he shall be last of all and servant of all."

Proverbs 25:6-7 (NASB) 6 Do not claim honor in the presence of the king, And do not stand in the place of great men; 7 For it is better that it be said to you, "Come up here," Than for you to be placed lower in the presence of the prince, whom your eyes have seen.

- Self-Importance in ministry

2 Corinthians 12:11 (TLB) You have made me act like a fool—boasting like this—for you people ought to be writing about me and not making me write about myself. There isn't a single thing these other marvelous fellows have that I don't have too, even though I am really worth nothing at all.

Slithering sermons of soft soap
Place Churches on steep slope

- Self-help (Productive, though weak)

2 Corinthians 11:30 (TLB) But if I must brag, I would rather brag about the things that show how weak I am.

B) Selective Biblical Reference In Self-Evaluation

- Self Interest (self-pity and Murmuring are of self-centered expression and are very harmful)

Exodus 16:3 (KJV) And the children of Israel said unto them, Would to God we had died by the hand of the LORD in the land of Egypt, when we sat by the flesh pots, and when we did eat bread to the full; for ye have brought us forth into this wilderness, to kill this whole assembly with hunger.

> Reflect on your reflections,
> Look for any complications

- Self-serving (Bad shepherds)

Ezekiel 34:2 (NASB) Son of man, prophesy against the shepherds of Israel. Prophesy and say to those shepherds, Thus says the Lord GOD, "Woe, shepherds of Israel who have been feeding themselves! Should not the shepherds feed the flock?"

- Selfishness and self-centeredness

Amos 6:6 (TLB) You drink wine by the bucketful and perfume yourselves with sweet ointments, caring nothing at all that your brothers need your help.

- Self-pity (leads to rebellion)

Numbers 16:12-13 (NIV) 12 Then Moses summoned Dathan and Abiram, the sons of Eliab. But they said, "We will not come! 13 Isn't it enough that you have brought us up out of a land flowing with milk and honey to kill us in the desert? And now you also want to lord it over us?"

- Self-pity and its variations (Have I not given you more than the other person?)

1 Samuel 22:7-8 (NIV)7 Saul said to them, "Listen, men of Benjamin! Will the son of Jesse give all of you fields and vineyards? Will he make all of you commanders of thousands and commanders of hundreds? 8 Is that why you have all conspired against me? No one tells me when my son makes a covenant with the son of Jesse. None of you is concerned about me or tells me that my son has incited my servant to lie in wait for me, as he does today."

- Being rebuffed by subordinates-evokes intense self-pity and anger

Esther 5:9-10 (TLB) What a happy man was Haman as he left the banquet! But when he saw Mordecai there at the gate, not standing up or trembling before him, he was furious.

- Self-pity of a so called Christian's question is, "is righteous living of no purpose?"

Psalms 73:12-13 (KJV) 12 Behold, these are the ungodly, who prosper in the world; they increase in riches. 13 Verily I have cleansed my heart in vain, and washed my hands in innocency.

- Blaming God is silly and self-pity is stupid

Jeremiah 20:7 (KJV)7 O LORD, thou hast deceived me, and I was deceived: thou art stronger than I, and hast prevailed: I am in derision daily, every one mocketh me.

Habakkuk 1:2-4 (TLB)[2] "Help! Murder!" I cry, but no one comes to save.3 Must I forever see this sin and sadness all around me? Wherever I look I see oppression and bribery and men who love to argue and to fight. 4 The law is not enforced, and there is no justice given in the courts, for the wicked far outnumber the righteous, and bribes and trickery prevail.

B) Selective Biblical Reference In Self-Evaluation

- Domestic self-pity

Luke 10:39-42 (KJV) 39 And she had a sister called Mary, which also sat at Jesus' feet, and heard his word. 40 But Martha was cumbered about much serving, and came to him, and said, "Lord, dost thou not care that my sister hath left me to serve alone? bid her therefore that she help me." 41 And Jesus answered and said unto her, "Martha, Martha, thou art careful and troubled about many things: 42 But one thing is needful: and Mary hath chosen that good part, which shall not be taken away from her."

- Jesus refuses sympathy and self-pity

Luke 23:27-28 (KJV) 27 And there followed him a great company of people, and of women, which also bewailed and lamented him. 28 But Jesus turning unto them said, "Daughters of Jerusalem, weep not for me, but weep for yourselves, and for your children".

- Self-dividing is self-destructive

Christians are the only religious group where, when someone else is identified as a Christian, asks immediately which church that person belongs to, whereas Hindus, Muslims Buddhists are satisfied that their neighbor is of the same religion!!

- Self-Righteousness is "I am holier than you" attitude; it is condemned by God

Luke 18:9 (NASB) And He also told this parable to some people who trusted in themselves that they were righteous, and viewed others with contempt.

- Self-deception

Galatians 6:3 (KJV) For if a man think himself to be something, when he is nothing, he deceiveth himself.

- Self-will is stubbornness

Exodus 32:9 (KJV) And the LORD said unto Moses," I have seen this people, and, behold, it is a stiffnecked people"

Deuteronomy 9:6 (NIV) Understand, then, that it is not because of your righteousness that the LORD your God is giving you this good land to possess, for you are a stiff-necked people.

- Self-perception

Psalms 19:12 (TLB) But how can I ever know what sins are lurking in my heart? Cleanse me from these hidden faults.

- Self-willed person will suffer 'stiff-neck' and 'hardening of the heart' both- fatal conditions

2 Kings 17:14 (KJV) Notwithstanding they would not hear, but hardened their necks, like to the neck of their fathers, that did not believe in the LORD their God.

Jeremiah 7:24 (NIV) But they did not listen or pay attention; instead, they followed the stubborn inclinations of their evil hearts. They went backward and not forward.

Nehemiah 9:16 (KJV) But they and our fathers dealt proudly, and hardened their necks, and hearkened not to thy commandments,

Isaiah 48:4 (KJV) Because I knew that thou art obstinate, and thy neck is an iron sinew, and thy brow brass;

Acts 7:51 (NASB77) You men who are stiff-necked and uncircumcised in heart and ears are always resisting the Holy Spirit; you are doing just as your fathers did.

B) Selective Biblical Reference In Self-Evaluation

Hebrews 3:7-8 (NIV) 7 So, as the Holy Spirit says: "Today, if you hear his voice, 8 do not harden your hearts as you did in the rebellion, during the time of testing in the desert,"
Self-indulgence is self-destructive

Some time ago, the History Channel came out with programs called the "Seven Deadly Sins". These are really the Ten Commandments minus the ones referring to our accountability to God, and the fourth commandment, referring to our obligation to the parents.

As mentioned earlier, when we come to the Cross, receive Jesus and the Holy Spirit into our lives, our inner spirit is born again and the light of God enters our hitherto dead, depraved, darkened spirit. As a result, most of the 'ugly' components of our 'self' begin to disappear. God works this 'salvage' process within us.

God does not take advantage of us even at this time to force us become what He wants us to be. He values our personal choices and provides opportunities for our will to permit our godly and good 'selves' to eliminate the other bad and ugly 'selves' by crucifying them and putting them to death. This is the process of sanctification. This is why self-abnegation, self-effacement, self-control, self-denial and self-sacrifice are given to us as tools for our will and choice. After these good 'tools' have served their purpose, they too must be surrendered to God at the altar of self-consecration. It is then that all our self will be crucified and put to death, replaced by our Lord Jesus totally. Then the mind-set of Jesus can be in us, enabling us to do the perfect will of God.

Our self, however good, is still depraved and septic compared to the holiness of Heaven and God. If we can make ourselves us fit to live with God in His holy Heaven for eternity applying our good and godly selves, there would have been no need for the Lord Jesus to come, suffer and die on the Cross for you and me. No one will be admitted or given an entrance into a sterile room as such, however well-dressed he or she may be; new shoes, arresting looks, fabulous hairdo are all of no avail. The feet, the entire body, the hair and the face have to be fully covered by sterile overalls. We understand and accept the fact that even the CEO or the owner of a hospital is not permitted to enter a sterile operation theater when a major surgery is being performed, unless he obeys the rules of the sterile procedures and dons the drab sterile overalls over his expensive dress. How much more should be the demands for holiness by God for entry into His eternal Holy Heaven? But Jesus has offered to us the robes of righteousness enabling us to have permission to enter Heaven, which is holy and eternal.

When there remains no 'self' in us, even the godly ones, and our 'selves' will not be there to claim the glory due only to Father God. We will live under His grace completely, with no self-effort to interfere with the perfect will and purpose of God.

James 1:23-25 (TLB) [23]For if a person just listens and doesn't obey, he is like a man looking at his face in a mirror; [24]as soon as he walks away, he can't see himself anymore or remember what he looks like.[2] [5]But if anyone keeps looking steadily into God's law for free men, he will not only remember it but he will do what it says, and God will greatly bless him in everything he does.

The BAD Self

- Self Esteem can lead to a dangerous deception. The so named protection of 'Loss of personal worth' is a subtle self-arrogance trying to challenge our accountability and responsibility. It teaches the art of learning the 'blame game', and how to dump one's own faults upon another.

There is a dangerous plethora of psychological deception, which has infiltrated and is dominating preachers, teachers, politicians and the judiciary claiming dependence upon self-worth, self-acceptance and self-esteem. This philosophy caters to the ego, the self and makes one 'self-centered'. Even kindergarten children are being brain warped by the 'educational centers' into this dangerous foolishness. The children are taught that Bible is not the ultimate truth, or the only moral yardstick, and that there are different points of view for the children to pick and choose. The kids are made to believe that they should be in charge, and be free to make their own choice. With the result, the children are becoming rebel-

B) Selective Biblical Reference In Self-Evaluation

lious, undisciplined and arrogant. They have started believing that they are worth so much that everyone has to give in to their every whim and fancy. They have lost respect for elders, especially the parents, whom they have come to believe, exist to serve them; and that the older generations have no sense of their own. The children are taught to turn their loving, caring parents into the grasping jaws of the law if the parents try to discipline them at home. This atrocity has become a law in many countries. Using this doctrine, psychologists, educational systems, the judicial systems and the government are maligning parental discipline and have outlawed the same at home! Hitler showed how children and adults alike could be brain washed, warped and controlled liked brainless robots to execute his wishes. His actions are being carried out even to this day in many 'so called' civilized nations!

- Self-esteem is foolish, dangerous and is not recommended

- Our self-esteem can be an abomination to God.

Luke 16:15 (KJV) And he said unto them, "Ye are they which justify yourselves before men; but God knoweth your hearts: for that which is highly esteemed among men is abomination in the sight of God."

- Only when you give up your self-esteem, you will admit to your wrongs

Zechariah 1:5 (TLB) Your fathers and their prophets are now long dead, but remember the lesson they learned, that God's Word endures! It caught up with them and punished them. Then at last, they repented. "We have gotten what we deserved from God," they said. "He has done just what he warned us he would."

- Self-esteem fights against becoming Christ centered and Christ dependent.

Job 9:21 (KJV) Though I were perfect, yet would I not know my soul: I would despise my life.

- Self-esteem and self-reliance are due to pride in humanity's alleged ability

Isaiah 5:21 (NASB) Woe to those who are wise in their own eyes and clever in their own sight!

- Self-esteem is because of pride

Jeremiah 9:23-24 (NASB) 23 Thus says the LORD, "Let not a wise man boast of his wisdom, and let not the mighty man boast of his might, let not a rich man boast of his riches; 24 but let him who boasts boast of this, that he understands and knows Me, that I am the LORD who exercises loving-kindness, justice and righteousness on earth; for I delight in these things," declares the LORD.

- Self-esteem—is a false trick mirror for human justification

Luke 16:15 (TLB) Then he said to them, "You wear a noble, pious expression in public, but God knows your evil hearts. Your pretense brings you honor from the people, but it is an abomination in the sight of God.

- Self-esteem: God's evaluation is not the same as our estimation of our own selves

Job 9:21 (TLB) And even if I am utterly innocent, I dare not think of it. I despise what I am.

B) Selective Biblical Reference In Self-Evaluation

Self-esteem

Proverbs 16:2 (KJV) All the ways of a man are clean in his own eyes; but the LORD weigheth the spirits.

Isaiah 5:21 (NASB) Woe to those who are wise in their own eyes and clever in their own sight!

- Self-esteem of gay bishops and clergy

Ezekiel 16:56-57 (TLB) 56 In your proud days you held Sodom in unspeakable contempt.

57 But now your greater wickedness has been exposed to all the world and you are the one who is scorned—by Edom and all her neighbors and by all the Philistines.
Such people will also say that if they had been in Eden, they would not have rebelled against God and joined up with Satan! (But sadly, many of them do not even believe in the Bible).
Humanity's estimation of "self" is different from God's evaluation

Proverbs 16:2 (NASB) All the ways of a man are clean in his own sight; But the LORD weighs the motives.

Proverbs 21:2 (NASB) Every man's way is right in his own eyes, But the LORD weighs the hearts.

- Self-confidence. Self-confidence does not put confidence in God, but upon self

2 Chronicles 12:1 (TLB) But just when Rehoboam was at the height of his popularity and power he abandoned the Lord, and the people followed him in this sin.

- Self-confidence is easily lost

Nehemiah 6:16 (NIV) When all our enemies heard about this, all the surrounding nations were afraid and lost their self-confidence, because they realized that this work had been done with the help of our God.

- In times of weakness, 'self' loses hope

Job 6:13 (TLB) For I am utterly helpless, without any hope.

- Self-confidence can lead to perversion

Job 9:20 (KJV) If I justify myself, mine own mouth shall condemn me: if I say, "I am perfect", it shall also prove me perverse.

- Boast only about God; not about your perceived achievements

Jeremiah 9:23-24 (TLB) 23 The Lord says: "Let not the wise man bask in his wisdom, nor the mighty man in his might, nor the rich man in his riches.24 Let them boast in this alone: That they truly know me, and understand that I am the Lord of justice and of righteousness whose love is steadfast; and that I love to be this way."

Self-assurance

Galatians 6:4 (KJV) But let every man prove his own work, and then shall he have rejoicing in himself alone, and not in another.

B) Selective Biblical Reference In Self-Evaluation

- Self-image and self-reliance often indicate pride, arrogance and rebellion

1 Samuel 2:3 (TLB) Quit acting so proud and arrogant! The Lord knows what you have done, and he will judge your deeds.

- When priests sin, they make people sin (Eli's rebellious self-indulging sons)

1 Samuel 2:23-25 (KJV) 23 And he said unto them, "Why do ye such things? For I hear of your evil dealings by all this people. 24 Nay, my sons; for it is no good report that I hear: ye make the LORD'S people to transgress."

Religion is the outer dress of the outer man, but God looks for what is deeper within in our inner man

- Self-confidence and self-reliance will fail when real test or trial comes

Mark 14:31 (NASB) But Peter kept saying insistently, "Even if I have to die with You, I will not deny You!" And they all were saying the same thing also.

- 'Self' lacks understanding

Psalms 32:9 (NIV) Do not be like the horse or the mule, which have no understanding but must be controlled by bit and bridle or they will not come to you.

- Self-gratification— Self is depraved from birth

Psalms 58:3-5 (KJV) The wicked are estranged from the womb: they go astray as soon as they be born, speaking lies.

- Self-incrimination — Self never fails to make an ass of itself

Proverbs 18:2 (NIV) A fool finds no pleasure in understanding but delights in airing his own opinions.

GOOD and GODLY Self

Why do we have to surrender and give up our good and godly selves?
When God who created each one of us, gave us Him-self
The least we can, is to crucify the desires of our flesh (self)
The different 'selves' with their deceitful desires, lusts, pride and the earthly nature within us make up our flesh.

Galatians 5:24 (KJV) And they that are Christ's have crucified the flesh with the affections and lusts.

Ephesians 4:22 (NIV) You were taught, with regard to your former way of life, to put off your old self, which is being corrupted by its deceitful desires

Colossians 3:5 (NIV) Put to death, therefore, whatever belongs to your earthly nature: sexual immorality, impurity, lust, evil desires and greed, which is idolatry.

1 Peter 4:2 (KJV) That he no longer should live the rest of his time in the flesh to the lusts of men, but to the will of God.

To become acceptable to God, even the matter part of us (our bodies) does matter

Romans 12:1 (KJV) I beseech you therefore, brethren, by the mercies of God, that ye present your bodies a living sacrifice, holy, acceptable unto God, which is your reasonable service.

We become acceptable through:

B) Selective Biblical Reference In Self-Evaluation

- Self-denial — earthly nature (our old self) needs to be put to death!

Colossians 3:5 (NASB) Therefore consider the members of your earthly body as dead to immorality, impurity, passion, evil desire, and greed, which amounts to idolatry.

Titus 2:12 (KJV) Teaching us that, denying ungodliness and worldly lusts, we should live soberly, righteously, and godly, in this present world

Luke 14:33 (KJV) So likewise, whosoever he be of you that forsaketh not all that he hath, he cannot be my disciple.

Matthew 10:38 (KJV) And he that taketh not his cross, and followeth after me, is not worthy of me.

- Self-denial is possible only when one is willing to be under God's control

Matthew 16:24 (KJV) Then said Jesus unto his disciples, If any man will come after me, let him deny himself, and take up his cross, and follow me.

- Taking up the cross is self-sacrifice, possible only when Christ replaces our "self"

Luke 14:27 (NASB) Whoever does not carry his own cross and come after Me cannot be My disciple.

- I, my, me and mine are the main expressions of "self"

Luke 14:33 So then, none of you can be My disciple who does not give up all his own possessions.

- Self-sacrifice is possible when we surrender our all to Him who gave us His all

"Crucifying flesh", does not mean maiming the 'outer body', but putting to death the fleshly desires of the person which are a part of our inner man.

Matthew 5:29-30 (KJV) 29 And if thy right eye offend thee, pluck it out, and cast it from thee: for it is profitable for thee that one of thy members should perish, and not that thy whole body should be cast into hell. 30 And if thy right hand offend thee, cut it off, and cast it from thee: for it is profitable for thee that one of thy members should perish, and not that thy whole body should be cast into hell.

- The attitude of our minds will have influence on our willingness to give up any component of our 'self'

Galatians 5:25 (TLB) If we are living now by the Holy Spirit's power, let us follow the Holy Spirit's leading in every part of our lives. Put off old self

Ephesians 4:23-24 (NIV) 23 to be made new in the attitude of your minds; 24 and to put on the new self, created to be like God in true righteousness and holiness.

- We are enabled to self-denial when the 'I' of our self bends (in obedience) to receive and retain 'C' Christ within; and, further bends to become 'S' in Submission to the will of the Father

Philippians 3:8 (NIV) What is more, I consider everything a loss compared to the surpassing greatness of knowing Christ Jesus my Lord, for whose sake I have lost all things. I consider them rubbish, which I may gain Christ

B) Selective Biblical Reference In Self-Evaluation

- Self-abnegation is to renounce, relinquish all importance given to one's self

- The Lord Jesus and Paul declared that they were nothing

John 5:30 (KJV) I can of mine own self do nothing: as I hear, I judge: and my judgment is just; because I seek not mine own will, but the will of the Father which hath sent me.

1 Corinthians 15:9 (NIV) For I am the least of the apostles and do not even deserve to be called an apostle, because I persecuted the church of God.

- Self-effacing by the powerful army commander

Luke 7:7 (NIV) That is why I did not even consider myself worthy to come to you. But say the word, and my servant will be healed.

- Self-sacrifice by the creator God Himself!

Philippians 2:5-7 (KJV) 5 Let this mind be in you, which was also in Christ Jesus: 6 who, being in the form of God, thought it not robbery to be equal with God: 7 But made himself of no reputation, and took upon him the form of a servant, and was made in the likeness of men:

- Self-sacrifice is possible when one has the mindset of Jesus to obey God

Genesis 22:11-12 (NIV) 11 But the angel of the LORD called out to him from heaven, "Abraham! Abraham!" "Here I am," he replied.12 "Do not lay a hand on the boy," he said. "Do not do anything to him. Now I know that you fear God, because you have not withheld from me your son, your only son."

- **Self-control is the ninth fruit of the spirit.**

It indicates a person should have:

1) A deep desire to do the will of God and fulfill the purpose for which he /she are created.
2) Have a goal for connecting with God through the Lord Jesus, and keep the connection through obedience to the Holy Spirit of God.
3) Be well focused. Athletic runners are focused at the finish line and to win the applause of people by winning the race. A Christian seeks to please God and see the approval in God's face as God says, "Well done, you faithful servant".
4) Have self-restraint: Every boxer must know what his weaknesses are. A runner in a race must gradually increase his speed and distance during training. During the race, he knows when to hold back, when to hold on and when to sprint all out. Every sportsperson needs adequate training and regular warm up, so that the muscles do not rupture or fatigue by sudden strain on them.
5) Have self-discipline: Self-discipline starts in the mind and heart with the question whether one really wants to register for the competition. If the desire in the mind and the intent of the heart are strong enough, it will be sustained with determination and endurance to persist until the completion of the task. Every serious athlete sacrifices pleasures and indulgences during the rigorous training for the sports event. It does not mean that the athlete loses the temptation to indulge in food or alcohol or sex. His or her urges are strong but the person will suppress them through self-control, choosing to do his or her best in the athletic event. A disciplined person does not get into any excess. Once the event is over, the suppressed desires explode into indulgence. Therefore, self-discipline is not the same as self-control. For, a few persons may apply self-restraint on some of their activities by their own will power of their minds. If they are able to overcome the clamoring of their bodily sensations and stay on course,

B) Selective Biblical Reference In Self-Evaluation

others consider them as great and extra-ordinary. Some of them, who are charismatic, become leaders of small or large groups. Sooner than later, their pride becomes too big for them to keep under control, and as common to all of us, their vanity overcomes their sanity. The "self" of humans have a tendency to migrate up and down with emotional waves, or, sideways, while trying to dodge the inevitable trials, which assail all humanity throughout our lives.

There is another kind of self-control. This is a great celestial gift. This type of self-control cannot be obtained unless there is peace with God. Peace with God brings peace within the mind of the person. This peace brings self-control, which was found in the "mind set of Jesus" and can be obtained only through Jesus. Jesus told His followers to go out into the world and make disciples, and gave them the power and authority to do so. Such a disciple is well disciplined having peace within, and power from God.

When the "Savior Jesus" replaces our "self", there will be no instability, with our violent emotions or any external raging of winds or the waves. For while we, as humans can only cry "please be still", if Jesus is really with us, He will say "peace, be still" and we will see that the winds and the waves will obey. When any one becomes Christ centered, self-control will follow automatically. This self-control comes from God through the Lord Jesus Christ dwelling within and it brings the body under God's influence as we submit the flesh and the body in obedience to His will.

- **Self-control starts with tongue control**

Psalms 39:1-2 (KJV) 1 I said, I will take heed to my ways, that I sin not with my tongue: I will keep my mouth with a bridle, while the wicked is before me.2 I was dumb with silence, I held my peace, even from good; and my sorrow was stirred.

- No one can be perfect unless the tongue is brought under God's control

James 3:2 (NASB) For we all stumble in many ways. If anyone does not stumble in what he says, he is a perfect man, able to bridle the whole body as well.

- Self (tongue) denial is given to help us from self-incrimination

Psalms 39:1 (KJV) I said, I will take heed to my ways, that I sin not with my tongue: I will keep my mouth with a bridle, while the wicked is before me.

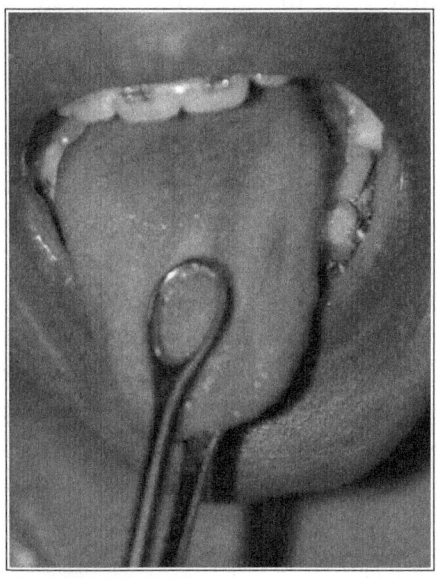

Tongs to restrain the Tong-ue

- Actions at times of crisis must not get us go 'out of control'

James 1:19-20 (NASB) 19 This you know, my beloved brethren. But everyone must be quick to hear, slow to speak and slow to anger;20 for the anger of man does not achieve the righteousness of God.

Proverbs 16:32 (NIV) Better a patient man than a warrior, a man who controls his temper than one who takes a city.

B) Selective Biblical Reference In Self-Evaluation

- Self-control includes avoiding gluttony

Proverbs 23:1 (TLB) When dining with a rich man, be on your guard and don't stuff yourself, though it all tastes so good; for he is trying to bribe you, and no good is going to come of his invitation.

- Self-abstinence is advocated to abstain from lust

1 Peter 4:2 (KJV) That he no longer should live the rest of his time in the flesh to the lusts of men, but to the will of God.
2 Peter 1:6 (NIV) and to knowledge, self-control; and to self-control, perseverance; and to perseverance, godliness;

- Self-control is. . .Practicing our will power and our choice to say 'no' to wrong desires

Titus 2:12 (NIV) It teaches us to say "No" to ungodliness and worldly passions, and to live self-controlled, upright and godly lives in this present age,

- Self-acceptance is to realize that God gave us life and that for a purpose

Psalms 139:13-16 (KJV) 13 For thou hast possessed my reins: thou hast covered me in my mother's womb. 14 I will praise thee; for I am fearfully and wonderfully made: marvellous are thy works; and that my soul knoweth right well. 15 My substance was not hid from thee, when I was made in secret, and curiously wrought in the lowest parts of the earth.16 Thine eyes did see my substance, yet being unperfect; and in thy book all my members were written, which in continuance were fashioned, when as yet there was none of them.

- Self-discovery should be to find our ID (Identification) in Jesus who died in our place.

1 Peter 2:9 (KJV) But ye are a chosen generation, a royal priesthood, a holy nation, a peculiar people; that ye should shew forth the praises of him who hath called you out of darkness into his marvellous light:

- Self-discipline is given to keep us from harmful self-indulgence

1 Corinthians 9:27 (KJV) But I keep under my body, and bring it into subjection: lest that by any means, when I have preached to others, I myself should be a castaway.
1 Peter 2:11 (KJV) Dearly beloved, I beseech you as strangers and pilgrims, abstain from fleshly lusts, which war against the soul;

- Self-determination is given us to have some power to resist temptation

Proverbs 23:31-32 (KJV) 31 Look not thou upon the wine when it is red, when it giveth his colour in the cup, when it moveth itself aright.32 At the last it biteth like a serpent, and stingeth like an adder.

- Self-restraint is given to us to enable us to have sexual restraint

1 Samuel 21:4-5 (TLB) 4 "We don't have any regular bread," the priest replied, "but there is the holy bread, which I guess you can have if only your young men have not slept with any women for a while." 5 "Rest assured," David replied. "I never let my men run wild when they are on an expedition, and since they stay clean even on ordinary trips, how much more so on this one!"

- Self-awareness is given to avoid evaluating others. God is the judge, and not you and I

Isaiah 64:6 (KJV) But we are all as an unclean thing, and all our righteousnesses are as filthy rags; and we all do fade as a leaf; and our iniquities, like the wind, have taken us away.

B) Selective Biblical Reference In Self-Evaluation

Galatians 6:1 (TLB) Dear brothers, if a Christian is overcome by some sin, you who are godly should gently and humbly help him back onto the right path, remembering that next time it might be one of you who is in the wrong.

- Self-abandon is given to have passion to strive for something better

Philippians 3:8 (NIV) What is more, I consider everything a loss compared to the surpassing greatness of knowing Christ Jesus my Lord, for whose sake I have lost all things. I consider them rubbish, that I may gain Christ.

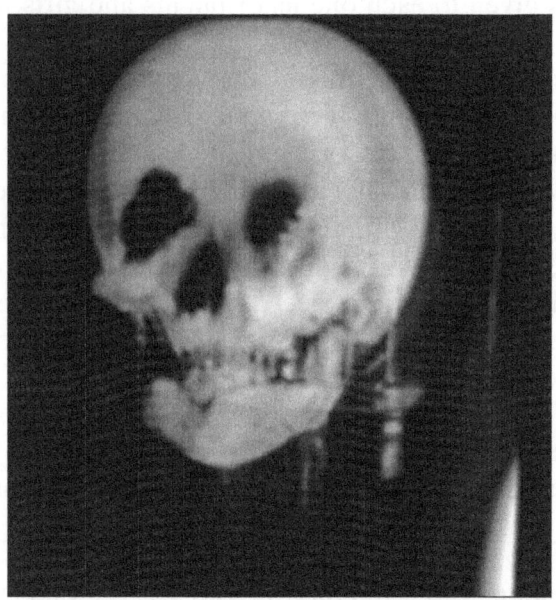

Self-evaluation to identify the syndromes afflicting you and me

C) What are my God given gifts or talents, and where are they now?

*G*od has given to each one us of talents and gifts to enrich our lives. How do we use them?

God has given many gifts (talents, strength) to each one of us. These can be classified into three columns: good, bad and ugly. We can really make the best use of them and benefit most when we handover our lives into God's hands by not only receiving Jesus into our hearts, but also making Him the Lord and Master of our lives. If we reject Jesus, our gifts will be taken over by evil spirits and fall into the Ugly column. Before we receive Jesus within, our gifts fall into the Bad column. When we receive Jesus into our lives our gifts will be in the good column.

Are our gifts in the GOOD, BAD or (heavens forbid) in the UGLY column?

Don't let your own strength sabotage or strangle you

The Good Self	The Bad Self	The Ugly Self
God controlled **God given gifts & talents**	**Human (self) controlled** The way we tend to use our talents	**Demon controlled** When we allow devils to control & abuse our talents

C) What Are My God Given Gifts Or Talents.....

Traffic green light [In life]	*Traffic Orange light [In life]*	*Traffic RED light [In life]*
Gentle	Soft	Weakling
Long suffering/ Patience	Tolerance	Indifference
Conscientious	Perfectionist	Petty Possessive, Demanding
Leadership	Driving/ dominating others	Despot-Tyrant
Servant Heart	Push over	Sucker-gullible
Carefulness	Hesitant	Fearful
Godly Messenger	Talkative	Gossip/slandering others
Communicator	Talkative Bore	Verbal diarrhea
Good Listener	Inquisitive / Interested Inquiring	Eavesdropper; itching ears
Discerning	Judgmental	Critical- Pharisee
Gourmet	Good appetite	Gluttony
Helpful	Interfering	Force (unwanted) help
Gallant	Gullible	Interferer
Cleanliness	Neat	Narcissus, obsessive
Quiet, Shy	Reserved	Unfriendly/ Recluse
Encourager	Flatterer	Con artist
Self-awareness	Self-esteem	Self-Centered
Sensitive	Get hurt easily	Self-pity & grudge-holder
Restful/Peaceful	Relaxing	Lazy
Contentment	Lack of goal	Drifter
Motivated	Hard worker	Idol worship (workaholic)

Business acumen	Wealth collecting	Miserly, grabber
Faith	Zealous	Fanatic-militant
Hope	Grope for hope	Dope depression
Thrifty	Tight-Fisted	Miserly
Relationship with God	Religious	Self-righteous
Feats—(gift of excelling)	Defeats. (Repeating mistakes)	Counter fetes/ Corruption
Strength	Show-off	Brutish-bully
Love	Affection	Lust
Determination	Obstinacy	Stubborn
Will power	Dominance	Dictatorial
Humility	Submissive	Gutless, cowardly
Courage	Daring bravado	Fool-hardy
Careful	Critical	Caustic condemning
Generous	Lavish	Decadent extravagance
Forceful	Demanding	Slave driver
Flexible/ Accommodative	Compromise	Corrupt
Zealous & Loyal	Jealous	Fanatic & Lunatic
Sweetness	Cloying Syrupy	Sickening
Friendly	Clinging	Co-dependent -Strangling
Hospitable	Good "host"	Partier
Gifted	Lifted(Applauded)	Drifter(Pride)
Outgoing	People pleaser(Popular)	Vain - Values lost self-pleaser

C) What Are My God Given Gifts Or Talents.....

Thrifty	Crafty	Stingly-misery, crooked
Peace maker	Administrator	Enforcer
Joyful	Happy	Giggly, silly
Faith in God	Faith in self in what "U" got	"U" Forgot Faith
Hope in God	Hope in self or group	Hope in 'soup'
Patience	Procrastination	Apathy/ Fatalism
Joyful sharer	Philanthropist	Corrupting briber

Let not your Strength become your Weakness

The science of psychiatry has ceased to be scientific and has succumbed to cultural changes as seen in their book of definition "DSM"

The 'politically correct' language is perversion of nomenclature, for it is 'doctoring' the dictionary which is a malpractice; it aims to cover a filthy litter with glitter - a trick mirror, or a coat of cover-up false mask.

Down the decades, the diseases have remained the same. Only the nomenclature is changed! Political / cultural mantles cover up the deadly germs treacherously.

The Bible calls it as	**Politically correct (corrupt) language calls it as**
Sin	Fun/freedom of expression/my right
Moral laws	Human right/ there are no absolutes
Sodomy, Lesbianism, Bestiality-perversion	Alternate life style/pursuit of happiness
Adultery	Consenting adults
Fornication	Practical Sex Education

God fearing people	Fanatics
Truth	Fools vocabulary, Hate -speech
Stealing	Relieving Fools of their burden (transferring assets)
Nonviolent peaceful Christians	Hate mongers. Proselytizers (audacious to convert others to nonviolent peaceful lives)
Murder - war - abortion	Selective population control. Cleansing (ethnic)
Responsibility	Unnecessary burden on one's life
Conviction	Unwanted and unnecessary guilt trip
Burden of sin	Guilt complex - to be removed by drugs or placated by psychology
Pollution of principles	Pluralism
Treachery, treason and lies	Political way of living
Saboteurs. Brain 'warpers'	News media/ pornography producers
Pornography	Educational Agenda for schools and colleges
Pride	Self esteem
Drug addiction	Freedom of expression, Pursuit of happiness
Grass — was cattle feed and for lawn	To make smoke to kill the lungs and brain
Pot — Vessels to cook food or keep water	Vapors made to fry the living brain
Right — Morally correct	To do whatever one likes to do; freedom
Freedom — from slavery/ shackles/oppression	To be free from moral obligations/accountability & responsibility

C) What Are My God Given Gifts Or Talents.....

There are questions we need to address; questions we should ask ourselves often, and answer truthfully. In such a case, when we ask God to forgive, heal and rectify, He will do it gladly every time. We have compiled for you a set of questions which are helpful, not exhaustive, but enough to stimulate our memories. For some of the questions, the answers may not be easy. God will reveal them in the appropriate time of our growth. Some questions are repeated, in order to gain a different perspective.

Bible is our guide, the Gold Standard, as well as the Yardstick for our lives.

God has given us Ten Simple basic Commandments. Do we want them? Do we obey them? Have we discarded them?

They are paraphrased as:-

1) We all have one and only God the Creator in spite of what we believe or do.
2) We are not to make any idols, including our 'self' to take the place of God.
3) We are not to abuse God's name by our words, actions or lives.
4) Give one in seven days to rest our body and mind, and to meditate on God.
5) Respect, obey and help our parents during their lives.
6) Should not hurt or kill others in our mind, with our 'lie' words or with our actions.
7) Should not commit sexual sins in our mind, or with our body.
8) Should not steal or take what we have not paid for. Must not become greedy.
9) Should not tell lies whether white, grey or black. Must not slander or gossip.
10) Should not covet what belongs to another, and avoid envy, and jealousy.

Commandments 1, 2, 3 and 4 are prophylactic to keep us in good health.

Commandments 5, 6, 7, 8, 9 and 10 are vital to save us from dangerous and deadly sickness affecting our physical and spiritual health causing death on earth and into eternity.

Take home points in self-evaluation

Do I host any of the Seven Deadly Sins the world talks about?

1) Hosting Sloth-laziness: gives a feeling of exhaustion, leading to depression and suicide.
2) Hosting Lust may be for wealth, power, possessions or sex.
3) Hosting Envy may be over what others possess
4) Hosting Anger, due to innate hostility, irritations, resentments and rage.
5) Hosting Pride, due to selfishness, and self-centeredness.
6) Hosting Greed - what does it profit a man who gains the whole world but loses his soul? Love of money is the root of all evil. Do not cover it up as thrift or prosperity.
7) Hosting Gluttony may be for certain food, drinks, sex, drugs or addictions. Lies/ slandering, false witness?

Self-evaluation (S.E) will satisfy the useful curiosity for knowledge within us

Do you not want to know who you are? (Who were your parents and ancestors?)

Do you not want to know what you are? (Human, demon, or 'demonoid')?

Do you not want to know where you are, and why?

Do you not want to know your personality and whether it can be improved?

Do you want to know your destiny?

Do you want to know your ultimate purpose for living?

Do you want to know God's desire for you?

Do you want to submit to God to lift you to your highest potential?

Biblical Self-confrontation (S.C.) for daily life and living

C) What Are My God Given Gifts Or Talents.....

S.C. and Religion

Am I a Christian, Muslim, Hindu, Buddhist, Atheist or an Animist?

In what way am I better than a person from another religion?

If I call myself a Christian why do I think so, or say so?

Was it because I was born to Christian parents, or got confirmed into a church?

Is it because I go to church, read the Bible or pray often?

S.C. and Faith

Do I know Jesus as my personal Savior?

Do I realize that I am a desperate sinner going to hell?

Do I realize that it was for my sins that Jesus was upon the Cross?

Have I realized and come to the Cross repenting for my sins and confessing them?

Did I receive forgiveness for my sins from the Lord whose Blood was shed for me?

Do I have the assurance that Jesus has come into my life and that my life belongs to Him?

Do I believe that by being in Jesus, I am granted eternal life with God?

Am I a follower of Jesus?

Am I a good sheep in following Jesus, or not?

Am I a good soldier in God's army, or not?

Do I agree that a soldier is not to ask why for an order, but be willing to do and to die?

Am I willing to be under strict physical and moral discipline?

Am I willing to forego my comforts and freedom?

Am I a good shepherd – of the flock, which really and wholly belongs to Jesus, not to me?

Do I go to church regularly and well prepared with prayer?

Why do I go? Is it a habit? Is it to meet folks? Is it because I am involved in church activities? Or, is it because I am involved with God?

If do not like going to church, why?

Do I read the Bible regularly?

Do I benefit every time I read the Bible? If not, why not?

Do I pray, and if I do, how often?

Muslims pray five times a day. Jews pray seven times a day. Buddhists and Hindus pray more than once a day. Most so called Christians go to their churches only on Sunday morning. This fact shows that Christians are the least religious.

The only hope for people of all religions is to come to the Cross of Jesus, repent, be forgiven, be connected to God, and follow the teachings of Jesus and share them with others.

The late Rev. James Kennedy had set up a questionnaire:

If you or I should die today, do I/you know that I/you will go to heaven.

If God asks me why He should let you/me into His heaven – what should you/I say?

To which each one must make an honest reply. What is your answer?

Do I talk about God and tell others about His gift of His Son? If not, why not?

Jesus has commissioned us to share the gospel with others in every part of the world.

What are your reasons for not doing it? You have to answer to God one day.

Do I talk with God? Alternatively, do I talk at God? Are my prayers petitions and applications like the grocery list covering personal needs and those of the closest ones?

Do I walk with God? Do I go where He leads me, or try to lead Him to where I want to go?

Will God go with me where I go? Do I trust God?

Is there daily private individual prayer as well as family prayer?

Is this prayer in the morning and for how long?

Is this prayer in the evening and for how long?

Do I insist on having family prayer every day?

Do I trust God to meet my need? Do I depend on my ability to work; or upon my bank account and savings; or my church, or charity, or my ability to earn or "take" from whereever?

God said love your neighbor. Family and friends are your neighbors. If you cannot love them, you cannot love God. Religion must

C) What Are My God Given Gifts Or Talents.....

imply a loving relationship with people and God. If not, religion can become useless or even dangerous.

S.C. for Preachers, teachers and educators
   Do I have any selfish motive or agendas in my attempt to teach or reach some one?
   Am I trying to fatten my wallet, or gain name and fame?
   Am I trying to build a mega organization (which will collapse within a few generations)?
   Am I trying to use my student or listener as a sword or an arrow to attack another?
   Am I giving vent to my own anger and violent nature, training another as a tool?
   Am I depicting God as merciful, or merciless by creating tools of destruction?
   Do I make it clear that murdering another is not the way to heaven?
   Do I make it clear that murder starts in the mind and is frequently carried out by mouth and then in action?
   Do I use love or anger, hate, greed and fear as my teaching or preaching curriculum?

S.C. for Home-dwellers
   Am I a good husband? What are my failures?
   Am I concerned enough to rectify problems at home?
   Am I a good father?
   Do I know what my children's ages, classes, interests, hobbies and who their friends are?
   Do I spend time in games and studies with my children?
   Do I teach the Bible and pray with the children every day?
   Am I a good role model for my children?
   Am I a good wife? How can I become a better one? What are my failures?
   What are my weak points?
   Am I a good mother?
   What are my weak points?
   Am I a good son?

What are my weak points?
Am I a good daughter?
What are my weak points?
Am I a good sibling?
What are my weak points?

S.C. at Work
Am I a good worker?
What are my weak points?
Do I take a storybook, newspaper, or electronic game to work?
Do I go to work on time and stay until the work time is over?
Do I take pride in doing my best at my work?
Do I accept correction about my work from my co-workers, bosses and 'inferiors'?
Do I put others in their 'places' when they try to advise me?
Do I flirt with anyone in the work area?
Do I swagger and act arrogantly in my work area?
Am I a good boss?
Do I care for people working under me?
Am I so interested in the work being completed, that I drive the workers hard?
Am I interested in helping the workers by personally assisting them in getting the work done?
Will I use any of the workers to inform me about the other workers?
Do I work side by side with the workers, or go for recreations, rest, or another job?
Am I a good steward?

S.C. at School or at College
Am I a good student?
Do I like to learn?
Do I like going to school/college?
Do I go late or get tardy often?
Do I do my homework well?
Do I date someone, or like to be popular with the other sex?
Am I a good teacher?

C) What Are My God Given Gifts Or Talents.....

Do I like to teach, or is it just a job?
Do I believe in what I teach, and try to follow the lessons I impart to others?
Do I love my students, and want the best for them?
Do I pray for my students, especially the difficult ones?
Do I want my students to surpass me in their lives?
What sort of role model am I?

S.C. and Social life
What sort of guest am I?
Am I a good host?
What are my addictions?
What are my hobbies?
How do I spend my leisure time? How much of time do I spend on rest and relaxation?

S.C. and Money management
How do I spend money?
How much is my income for a month?
How much is my savings at the end of the month?
How much do I give to God every month?
How much do I spend on my hobbies every month?

S.C. and Time management
How do I spend my time?
What are my working hours every day?
How much of time do I spend with my friends?
How much of time do I spend sleeping?
How many hours do I give to God every day?
How many hours do I spend on my hobbies every day?
How many hours do I spend watching TV or reading storybooks?
Do I keep my appointments?
Am I in time – punctual for my appointments?

Keeping correct time for any appointment is as important as keeping one's word. When we do not go to the doctor's office at the appointed time, we lose the opportunity of being seen that day, unless some other patients cancel their appointment for that day. When a litigant does not keep the appointment in the judicial court, his or her case may be lost. If we take our own time to catch a train or plane, we may have to pay again for our delay. People have made prior commitments of their time, and whenever we delay our appointed time with them, we cause major problems for them, in addition to being promise breakers. In Japan, people are punctual to a minute, so that they do not cause inconvenience to others. I used to be tardy and late for my appointments in the past, and before I became 'late Johnson', a non-Christian friend showed me my shortcoming and helped me to rectify this.

Is there any innate hostility in my behavior?
Do I get irritated, annoyed or angry easily?
Do I explode or simmer in anger?
Do I use harsh, critical or abusive words? Do I shout?
Do I dislike those who are opposed to my ideas, or consider them my enemies?
Do I dislike or can I barely tolerate some people?

q   Do I barely put up with my parents? Why
q   Do I stay away from my brothers or sisters? Why?
q   Am I indifferent to my siblings? Why?
q   I can tolerate my in-laws, wife, or husband only for a short time; why?

Do I avoid any of my family members? Why?
Do I avoid any friend? Why?
Do I apologies to those to whom I had been unkind in my thought, words or actions?
Do I remember a fight or a hurt for 1yr / 5yr / 10yrs or over?
Do I keep grudges within me and go over and over them at given opportunities?
Do I apologize or say sorry to my enemies or those with whom I had quarreled?
Do I forgive my enemies regardless of whether they reciprocated?
Who are my enemies?

C) What Are My God Given Gifts Or Talents.....

There is a wrong current 'catch phrase' which says "love your-self, and you must forgive your-self" in order to be happy in life. The truth is other-wise. If we are honest, we will realize that we are our worst enemies. It is only when we forgive others that God brings forgiveness and happiness into us.

Forgiving another should bring us freedom; if not, we had not really forgiven. If we refuse to forgive, we torture ourselves, as we lose our peace. When we lose our peace with others, we lose our peace with God. When we lose our peace with God, we lose peace within our own 'selves'.

Do I appreciate or feel glad when my 'difficult' colleague is promoted or honored?

Do I speak out or keep thinking of the bad that person has done?

> Every day as we look at the mirrors
> May God take away all our errors
>
> Sand to become glasses over the eye seems mystique
> But less brittle are the ones made of plastic
> However, both are of no use to our eyes
> If our blindness we can't realize

We have miles of blood vessels in the body. However, it is only the few inches of blood vessels in the heart or in central brain that play a major role in establishing whether one will have a heart attack or a stroke.

Self-confrontation for you and me personally

Do I keep my word?

Do I make promises? If I do, do I honor them always?

Do I make foolish promises?

A person's worth is as good as the person's word. This applies in every aspect of life, including marriage vows and simple statements of day-to-day promises. Our promises should not be like looking at the mirror, and forgetting how the face looks like soon after. If we do not keep our words, it would amount to lying noise coming out of our mouths.

Do I 'curry favor' of some because they are rich or famous or may include me in their will?

Do I want others to do what I want them or tell them to do?

Do I tell people that God wants them to do what I had told them? (If it is not God's will, it can harm instead of bringing joy. As we saw earlier, a good prophet who believed the words of another lying prophet was killed). There are many false prophets around, and we need to be careful.

Do I deny my well-wishers the freedom to criticize my children? Why?

Am I a 'sad-u-see'?

Who is a sad-u-see?

Am I a 'far-is-he'?

Who is far? Is it he, or me?

Am I free with advice? (Advice usually works otherwise - adds to vice on both sides - unless drenched and saturated with love and prayer.)

Do I give away what I do not use, or cannot use e.g.:- advice?

Do I receive advice gladly?

Do I receive correction from an equal, or one below me?

Am I willing to learn, or do I have a learning disability? (Remember, God had to correct and save a prophet of God through his own donkey.)

Do I have humility to learn from an ass or do I insist and persist in an asinine way?

Am I glad (proud) that I am being simple and humble? An oxymoron!

S.C. and trustworthiness

- q With money God has given me.
- q With money that I handle that belongs to others
- q With wife, sister, or daughter of another person
- q With another person's research work or labor
- q With my time
- q With the time for which I am paid by someone else

C) What Are My God Given Gifts Or Talents.....

q   Does my behavior and work change or improve with boss near or around me?

S.C and Personality profile

Am I Dominant; or Influential and Charismatic; or Critical; or Shy and Withdrawn?

(These are the four major groups of personalities, having in each, friendly or hostile personality).

Do I play or sing to a stage or the audience? Do I worship, or perform?

q   At work
q   At church
q   When in a company (Pharisee)

Do I wash other's feet, or lick their boots? If so, is it really in humility or fawning?
Have I a silent tongue and a sound mind?
When I come in, do I bring peace or war?
When I leave, do I leave behind peace or pieces?
When I give, what do I expect?
Do I want to be a leader?
Do I want to be the head and not a tail?
Then again,
Am I a 'tale'—bearer?
Do I 'share' secrets and prayer burdens of people with a third party without permission?
Am I a predator (often or now and then)?
Are my eyes that of a predator?
Is my tongue that of a predator?
What type of predator am I?
What am I consuming?
Why am I consuming?
Who am I consuming?
What is consuming me? Anger? Sex? Lust? Jealousy? Hatred? Hurts?

Am I a prey? (One who does not pray, or fails to study the Bible becomes an easy prey.)

Am I happy when guests come suddenly without getting my permission?

Do I try to buy blessing from God by a process of Seed Planting?

Do I reciprocate love or expect favors to be returned by the recipient?

(This is not giving, but bargaining, a business deal—where you may get a good deal, discount, or make a "kill" like winning the lottery)

Do I tell others that I have donated what I had given, and to whom?

Why did I tell that person?

- q   To improve my image
- q   To degrade the receiver's image
- q   To get some gain out of it
- q   Because I have a joint account
- q   To get a tax break

Do I pass on a secret in secret?

Do I try to give an impression as a better person than I really am?

Do I have self-pity? Do I seek sympathy from people?

Do I enjoy prayer and Bible reading or just do it?

Am I really born again?

If I am born again, what is the level of my growth and maturity?

Am I retarded, mal-developed or under-developed physically, emotionally or spiritually?

- q   Is my spiritual intake 'baby food' or spoon feeding?
- q   Do I have control over my output – Urinating? Bowel movement? Talking?
- q   Am I still in the stage of instant gratification?

C) *What Are My God Given Gifts Or Talents.....*

- q Do I have the Strength for walking upright? To help others and serve God?
- q Am I running the race to win, or being carried by others, whose time I am wasting?

Do I have a sense of humor?
Do I make a joke of others?
Who is the butt ends of my jokes?
Do I enjoy it when others make fun of me?
Spiritually am I like a crow – beating the air as I fly up? Do I believe in works to make me acceptable?
Spiritually am I like the eagle that uses the strength of the air to soar high in the sky? Do I trust in the air holding me up and use His grace to fly higher and higher?
Have I surrendered my all to God, and trust Him fully? Am I ready to trust Him fully so that I can abandon my safety and draw closer to Him as eagles do?
How do faith, hope, and love operate in my life?
Am I always conscious that disobeying God's words is worse than running through a red light in a busy intersection at peak traffic hour?

Who are my friends?
"Show me your friends and I will tell you your character" applies to all of us except to Jesus Christ who seeks out the vilest sinner, offers to forgive him / her, cleanse and then be a constant friend, guide and God.
Do I forgive my family or friends?
Do I forgive myself or justify myself?
Do I truly forgive others, or talk about others, and how they hurt me?
Do I forget the broken relationship incidents, or keep raking them up?
Do I lend frequently?
How do I get back what I loan?
Do I borrow, and how often?
Do I return it each time in time?

Do I have something that belongs to another?
Do I want something that belongs to another?
Do I think opportunities should be 'grabbed' up?
Do I think might is right and the end justifies the means?
Do I think meekness is weakness?

Do I demean, or criticize or accuse or speak badly about someone?

The finger pointing sign never fails. When the index finger accuses someone, three fingers accuse you. The thumb has to meet God for judgment.

Do I realize that our children are microphones with loud speakers attached? What I whisper at home, the children will proclaim it aloud in their lives as they grow up.

Do I realize that our children also act as the mirrors of our error-filled life as they grow up? Adam and Eve were convinced by Satan that God had lied to them about death, and that they will be like gods when they disregarded God's warning. God had told them that their defiant action will bring upon them death. Adam and Eve saw death of their offspring before their own death.

PART 3

A) Am I salt of the New Testament, or the pillar of salt of the Old Testament?

Jesus has asked us to be **Salt** and **Light** to the world
Self-Evaluation:-
Am I the salt Jesus wants me to be?
Alternatively, am I the pillar of salt in the Old Testament? (Lot's wife)

Matthew 5:13-14 Ye are the salt of the earth: but if the salt have lost his savour, wherewith shall it be salted? It is thenceforth good for nothing, but to be cast out, and to be trodden under foot of men. Ye are the light of the world. A city that is set on a hill cannot be hid.

Mark 9:50 Salt is good for seasoning. But if it loses its flavor, how do you make it salty again? You must have the qualities of salt among yourselves and live in peace with each other.

Seven good Functions of Salt—7 Up!

1. Salt gives flavor and taste

To give flavor and taste to the food (the bread of heaven).
Our individual lives, and not just our mouths should proclaim to everyone that our God provides tasty and nourishing food. Our

life style should invite others 'to taste and see how good our Lord is'. There is a moral and spiritual famine all around us. People eat anything they come across in order to stay alive. They are unaware that some of the foods they eat are poison weeds and roots, which are addictive, hurtful to their bodies, minds and soul and ultimately lead to their premature death. Christians need to share the life giving wonderful bread of heaven with others, and act as the flavoring salt of heaven to the bread of life from heaven. Christ must become our main food for our nourishment health and life.

Job 6:6 (NIV) Is tasteless food eaten without salt, or is there flavor in the white of an egg?

Jesus asked us to be 'salt' for the earth - to add to good taste and flavor of food.

2. Salt preserves food

To preserve food (His word), the Bread from heaven
Salt is a good preservative. It prevents putrefaction of the flesh of animals, birds and even fish. Foods are spoilt quickly when adequate salt is not added .In a society where the morals begin to decay, Christians are to be the salt, preserving agents preventing moral decay and putrefaction.

John 6:33 (NIV) For the bread of God is he who comes down from heaven and gives life to the world.

Do I preserve His Word in my heart and life?

3. Salt creates thirst

To create thirst (Thirst for the Word), the water of life.
A proverb says 'you can only take the horse to water, but you cannot make it drink!' However, those who know about the properties of salt can create thirst in the horse by putting salt crystals in its

mouth, under its lip, and, the salty taste will make the horse to drink very soon.

Jer 2:13 (NIV) O LORD, the hope of Israel, all who forsake you will be put to shame. Those who turn away from you will be written in the dust because they have forsaken the LORD, the spring of living water."My people have committed two sins: They have forsaken me, the spring of living water, and have dug their own cisterns, broken cisterns that cannot hold water."

Is my life lived as salt, so as to create a thirst for God and His Word in my neighbors?

4. Salt quenches thirst

To quench thirst – we will never thirst again for drinks which are hazardous to our health.
People are thirsting. We are like people who are adrift on a raft on the ocean. We find water in the ocean unfit to drink; it causes us to become sick or even die if we do drink it. We are like the travelers on foot in the hot Sahara desert, a hot world that lacks the moisture of kindness and compassion. Christians are not to offer their personal saltiness to the needy but are to become clean conduits from Christ, who is the fountain and the river of pure sweet, life- giving water.

John 6:35 (NIV) Then Jesus declared, "I am the bread of life. He who comes to me will never go hungry, and he who believes in me will never be thirsty."

Am I a clean conduit pipe for the water of life to flow through, to quench the thirst of many, or am I contaminating the water from God?

5. Salt is needed for sweat loss

To combat sweat loss- from dehydration & desiccation [of compassion]

We live in a dry land full of quarrels, war, hatred, greed, and selfishness. Whatever little human kindness there is, evaporates when it affects one's self. People think that water will do the trick. However, if the salt that goes out of their body is not replaced, people will become sick or die. Death due to heat stroke and sunstroke are due to salt depletion and electrolyte imbalance. Christians are to be the salt that would replenish people's need.

Ex. 17:3 (NIV) But the people were thirsty for water there, and they grumbled against Moses. They said, "Why did you bring us up out of Egypt to make us and our children and livestock die of thirst?"

Do I cause a dehydrating environment upon my neighbors by my hot temper, or do I share the Living Water offered by the Lord Jesus?

6. Salt has healing property

As saline solution used in surgery; eg-in God's operations (surgical procedures) and for Healing of wounds.

Most of the surgical procedures whether minor or major, will not be started without an intra-venous infusion of saline (0.9% salt-solution).

Ezek 16:4 (NIV) On the day you were born your cord was not cut, nor were you washed with water to make you clean, nor were you rubbed with salt or wrapped in cloths.

Salt is an anti-septic (kills many harmful germs and bacteria). Salt is an astringent. Due to its high osmolality, it draws out the edema fluid from open wounds and helps in rapid healing. A paste of Salt and glycerin are applied to suck out septic material and pus from abscesses. Every Christian needs to be the healing salt.

Do I allow God to use me as saline solution during His operations for many and as an Anti-septic agent?

7. Salt is a covenant symbol

As a covenant (bond) between God and humankind; as well as among humankind.
For centuries, people in the middle and far Eastern countries had used salt as a precious trading commodity as well as a token for relationship, trust and truce, binding people together for many generations.

Lev 2:13 (NIV) Season all your grain offerings with salt. Do not leave the salt of the covenant of your God out of your grain offerings; add salt to all your offerings.

Num 18:19 (NIV) Whatever is set aside from the holy offerings the Israelites present to the LORD I give to you and your sons and daughters as your regular share. It is an everlasting covenant of salt before the LORD for both you and your offspring.

Salt decreases the melting temperatures of ice and liquefies ice into water. Salt is therefore used for "de-icing" the slippery path and to help us to walk steadily without slipping and getting our bones broken. Even the roads are kept from getting icy, slippery, and hazardous by salting the roads. Aircraft and runways also need to be de-iced. Planes cannot take off when frozen and covered with ice. During landing and takeoff things can become treacherous, when the runway is icy or loaded with snow.
Do I have a personal covenant relationship with God through Jesus, allowing God to use me in whatever way He chooses to?

Seven Malfunctions of SALT - 7 Down.

1. Excess-salt makes food too salty. No one can savor any flavor or taste food.

Many Christians like to leave their scent on others, like animals that enjoy marking their 'turf and territory'. When God gives them a short 'message' to convey to others, they tend to convert it into a major 'massage' session trying their own methods of rubbing it in, and in the process, the message is lost, and the people are often hurt and bruised by the massage.

2. Excess salt starts one gagging, causing difficulty in swallowing.

Excess of one's self (salt) is hard for others to swallow however good, tolerant or close they may be. No sugar or syrup will make it easy for others to swallow 'you'. If, and when you try to feed on your own saltish self (pride and ego-diet), you yourself will choke to death. It is of interest to know that our own unruly tongue falls back during drunken stupor and during an anesthesia, and unless the tongue is pulled forward, it will cause death by closing our airway.

3. If excess salt is ingested (swallowed), it causes diarrhea.

Many varieties of salts are used to overcome constipation in people. The salt, because of it high osmolality (hypertonic nature) draws fluid into the bowel (intestines) from the blood supplying the walls of the intestines. The excess bulk of fluid in the bowels will loosen the stools and expel them as loose motion or diarrhea. Mere lip service indicates a more pathetic condition called as verbal diarrhea!

4. Excess salt in the blood leads to hypertension (high-blood pressure) with all its complications. The increase of salt within, causes fluid from the surrounding tissue to be drawn into the blood vessels, increasing the volume of blood and the blood pressure. Pride causes fluctuations of emotions, and plays havoc with the blood pressure.

5. Excess salt damages the kidneys, and pickles the viscera (internal organs like liver, kidneys etc). Kidney is essential for removing the toxic waste from the body. Retention of physical and spiritual waste products is fatal to the body as well as the soul.

6. Excess salt retention leads to fluid retention and edema (fluid enters into tissues) Fluid when entering into the lung, can cause suffocating, drowning death. Excess fluid retention causes swelling of not only the body, but also the mind. Swelling in the brain can cause coma and death.

7. When salt loses its savor, it is not even fit to be a fertilizer, but becomes a waste.

Mat 5:13 (NIV) You are the salt of the earth. But if the salt loses its saltiness, how can it be made salty again? It is no longer good for anything, except to be thrown out and trampled by men.

Christians are catechists and meant to act like catalyst. We should be only the trace of salt to flavor. The food offered to the needy, should be the bread of heaven and the water from the river of life. We should not deplete the "salt" our 'selves' by avoiding involvement, nor, should we present an excess of our 'selves'. We should only be the flavoring salt in heaven's banquet offered by God to the starving humankind. As John the Baptist said, "He (Jesus) should increase and I (we) should decrease."

Salt is a product obtained by the combination of two elements, namely the metal called Sodium and a very poisonous gas called Chlorine.

We are like the Chlorine gas, which is poisonous and lethal.

Masses of people were put to painful death in Chlorine chambers by tyrants! We are full of the poison of sin, and we carry death to ourselves and to others.

Water is normally used to put out fire. Sodium is a unique metal, which will burn and produce 'light' when dropped into water. The Sodium gives itself up as light, when surrounded by water, which normally puts out fire and light. Jesus came into the worldly atmosphere of sin, darkness and death, to give Himself up as the Light.

When Sodium acts upon Chlorine, it changes the poisonous material Chlorine into, 'Sodium-chloride'- the essential 'salt'.

When Jesus enters the heart and life of sinners who are like Chlorine, He transforms us into becoming "salt for others on earth". Therefore, we can function both as 'Light' and as 'Salt'.

Matthew 5:13-14 Ye are the salt of the earth: but if the salt have lost his savour, wherewith shall it be salted? it is thenceforth good for nothing, but to be cast out, and to be trodden under foot of men. Ye are the light of the world. A city that is set on an hill cannot be hid. Mark 9:50 Salt is good for seasoning. But if it loses its flavor, how do you make it salty again? You must have the qualities of salt among yourselves and live in peace with each other.

To summarize-

God asked us to be the salt of the earth.

- q To flavor nourishment – to apply His Word for all that we take in, or do.
- q To decrease your 'self', so that He may increase.
- q To preserve food and good things – to serve His word and keep it on our dining table.
- q To create thirst – to put concentrate of His word into others mouth to create thirst.
- q To quench thirst – drink His word , so we never thirst again for the world
- q To combat fluid loss –by drinking His word copiously and sharing our witness
- q To fertilize soil – sow His word wherever we go, so that plants will yield fruits

Do not get too salty (do not become a religious fanatic, who has no love for others)

- q Do not push into the mouth, doctrine which will choke and create gagging
- q Do not develop hypertension with anger and hate.
- q Do not retain past hurts and grudges— Edema or fluid retention
- q Do not slander others or develop verbal-diarrhea

q   Do not produce high blood pressure in others by your behavior.

We should decrease,
(so that)
God would increase
Am I being the salt God wants me to be?
How can I be the salt God wants me to be? Am I too salty, too full of 'self'?
Do I decrease so that God may increase? Does that not mean that I have to die to my 'self' and that self has to be replaced by the savior Jesus, who died for me and is risen to become the SON of righteousness, the Living Water and the Bread of Life to meet all one's needs.
God has asked us to be 'light' as well as to be 'salt'.

B) What kind of Light am I?

Wind chasers

The unshielded candle flame will bend, and try to follow any puff of wind, resulting in the light to be 'gone with the wind'

Hurricane Lamp Carriers

God may give to every child of His, a shelter for the Light He puts within. This protection is comparable to the transparent glass, which protects the flame from being put off by even strong winds. These lamps were called as Hurricane Lamps. The oil is poured into the metal base with air tight lid. A wick extends from the oil-containing base and is lit to provide light. The wick can be raised or lowered, to provide more or less brightness, by means of a screw wheel. The lamp has handles to make it safe and portable.

A self-dependent enlightened person is comparable to an oil lamp or an unshielded candle

Many unstable Christians allow their self to become important, even in serving God. Christians who do not allow the 'self' to dominate however, will humble themselves, seeking to do only what God wants him or her to do. However good our intentions are, our self is like the wick. The oil lamp has a limited container, with a wick dipping into it and the other end of the wick above the oil is lit. When we try to do more for God, the "wick" is turned up more. Things are brighter for a short while. Soon the extra "wick" starts emitting smoke, which tends to get deposited on the inside of the glass casing. If the inside and outside of the glass casing is not carefully and frequently cleaned, thick black soot heavily coats the inside of the glass casing, filtering off the light entirely. Quite a few born again, enlightened people have this "self" problem.

Torch carriers and torchbearers

There is a limited power stored in these batteries, or the oil soaked on it. People need to replenish the energy at frequent intervals, failing which we will be like the foolish torch bearing virgins in the parable related by Jesus.

Can the light of a Christian flicker, and why?

When a person's soul and spirit get connected to the Spirit of God, the enlightenment reveals the potential dangers of certain sensations and the harm that can be inflicted on the subject. Nevertheless the flesh, which had unrestricted indulgences of wrong and dangerous sensations hitherto, does not want to listen to the input by the now enlightened inner man. The soul, which carries the conscience like the germinating part of the seed, also carries the power to heed to the now enlightened spirit or to give in to the clamor of the flesh for its indulgence. Yes, the power of deciding is still ours. Whenever the decision is in favor of the Spirit, the light is on, and when the favor is to satisfy the flesh, there is disconnection from God's Spirit, and the light and the power are off, bringing in darkness.

When this connect and disconnect are repeated, the light begins to flicker, which hurts the eyes of the subject, as well as that of the neighbors. Some people develop epileptic seizures when exposed to flickering light. My father had a flickering torch light; he saw a big scorpion, and tried to avoid it. The torch light flickered out and my father could not see. He put his foot down away from where he had last seen the scorpion. However, the scorpion had moved in the darkness close to my father's foot. The scorpion stung him and nearly killed him with the potent painful venom. It is better not to have a flickering light, as there is an increased blindness experienced after a bright light suddenly goes off. After receiving the divine connection, many Christians flicker as they are 'torn between two loves' as the battle in their "double-minded" mind is waged between their pleasure seeking flesh and the now enlightened inner man.

James 1:8 (KJV) A double minded man is unstable in all his ways.

Flickering lights offer more hindrance than help. This is the reason why unstable Christians are the greatest danger to true Christianity.

B) What Kind Of Light Am I?

The New Testament life is meant to be like a light bulb, lit by constant electric power supply

Our soul is like the filament in an electric light bulb, which will flicker badly and blow the thin filament, or blow the fuse if there is significant and persistent electrical fluctuation. The bulb with a burnt-out filament will be of no use, as it cannot give light, even though its outer glass shell may be intact and appear to be good. Yes, we need our souls to be transformed by submission to God in order to glow with the divine light.

Electric power fixtures

When any individual human spirit does not, or has not connected with the (Celestial Power Line) Light of the Divine Spirit, the evil spirits will automatically take over control of the weaker human spirit. The evil spirits use the physiological pleasure sensations (flesh) of the inner body, plus the desires of the mind to control our souls and our weak human outer man's spirits. God can make the inner man's human spirit to be born again by connecting our inner man with the celestial power line of God's Light, enlightening our inner man's spirit. Our inner spirit is then 'liberated' from the rule of the evil spirits. However, God still gives to us the choice of using the switch for allowing the connection with the Divine Light to operate on our human mind. The good news however is that if and when we fail, we can penitently seek our God and He will forgive, and fix the blown fuse. God will salvage and save each seeking human. Our natural inner-man is a sinner-man, for spiritually it is in darkness.

The evil spirits are creatures of darkness. We all are living in spiritual (sin) darkness, surrounded by sin, whereas God is holy and 'Light' '. Only when we invite His Light (Jesus) to come into our hearts will our spirits receive the faith in our inner-man (and be enlightened by God). We cannot create 'light' within us by our own wisdom, knowledge, social works or good-deeds.

Light House

The Son of God will change our nature. We have the opportunity to transmit the Light of our Lord Jesus to help others who are groping in darkness. We are meant to be reflecting mirrors of God's countenance and His Light, beaming His light into our dark surroundings, helping others to find their way. That means that we are to be focused upon God. He can use us as a lighthouse.

Matthew 5:14 Ye are the light of the world. A city that is set on a hill cannot be hid.

PART 4

❋

This features great and small people of the Bible and the problems they faced because of the 'self' in them.

Try Self-examination, using the Bible to reveal both open and hidden Spiritual Dysfunctions and Syndromes.

Definition of Syndromes: - A group of medical signs and symptoms may point to the main underlying disease. Some of the signs and symptoms may overlap many diseases. For example in cancer of the lung, in Tuberculosis of the lung and many other different lung diseases, cough, sputum, and fever may be the common symptom. By evaluating the different signs and symptoms, and adding some 'tests', we can arrive at the diagnosis of the underlying disease. In medical dictionary, we use the word 'syndromes', which mean a collection of 'signs and symptoms' covering-up the patient's underlying disease. We will evaluate the signs and symptoms of spiritual dysfunctions and disease as 'syndromes' which require the Celestial Cosmic Mirror.

We are just beginning to check for the increase, decrease or depletion of neuro-chemicals in the brain, and associate them with diseases and disorders of the brain, their effect on our emotions, attitudes and behaviors. Though our nerve impulses have electro chemical conduction, there is no way to identify our problems when they are spiritual and non-material.

Each one of us hosts one or more syndromes documented in the Bible. The lives led by the 'self', or otherwise subjected to the Supreme God are described in the Bible to enlighten and educate us. Honest self-evaluation will help us in diagnosing the self, taking up the steering wheel and seeking to remedy things.

The following syndromes involves many stalwarts of the Bible with sterling characters. However, being human, they had faults and problems, which are truthfully documented in the scripture. These people became heroes in spite of their faults and problems because they sought Cosmic aid to see them through their trials in life. Studying their errors is not meant to decry or demean them, but to help us to seek help from above when we suffer from similar syndromes.

1) Aaron Syndrome

Bible reference

Exodus 32:1-6 (NIV) 1 When the people saw that Moses was so long in coming down from the mountain, they gathered around Aaron and said, "Come, make us gods who will go before us. As for this fellow Moses who brought us up out of Egypt, we don't know what has happened to him." 2 Aaron answered them, "Take off the gold earrings that your wives, your sons and your daughters are wearing, and bring them to me." 3 So all the people took off their earrings and brought them to Aaron. 4 He took what they handed him and made it into an idol cast in the shape of a calf, fashioning it with a tool. Then they said, "These are your gods, O Israel, who brought you up out of Egypt." 5 When Aaron saw this, he built an altar in front of the calf and announced, "Tomorrow there will be a festival to the LORD." 6 So the next day the people rose early and sacrificed burnt offerings and presented fellowship offerings. Afterward they sat down to eat and drink and got up to indulge in revelry.

Exodus 32:21-24 (NIV) 21 He said to Aaron, "What did these people do to you, that you led them into such great sin?" 22 "Do not be angry, my lord," Aaron answered. "You know how prone these people are to evil. 23 They said to me, 'Make us gods who will go before us. As for this fellow Moses who brought us up out of Egypt, we don't know what has happened to him.' 24 So I told them, 'Whoever has any gold jewelry, take it off.' Then they gave me the gold, and I threw it into the fire, and out came this calf!"

Situation assessment

Aaron was not an ordinary push over person. He was the mouth piece for Moses; he was with Moses when God took them through the confrontation with Pharaoh - all high risk encounters.

He was a mature man and second only to Moses in leading God's own people through the Red Sea. Yet when Moses had gone up Mt. Sinai for an extended period, Aaron aided and abetted the rebellion of some Israelites against Moses and God.

Why? His fickle faith was upon Moses the man of God, and not upon God the Master of Moses. When Moses was not around, Aaron was intimidated easily and wanted to keep his popularity and power. Many Christians follow their leader, for their trust is upon their mortal, fallible leader, and not on God. When their leader faints or falls, they all fall, with some wanting to take over leadership. Such people really belong to a cult, and not to God, who can make them triumph over trials and temptations.

When confronted by Moses, Aaron did not acknowledge his sin but tells foolish tales to excuse himself. Each father in the house and priest in the church or temple is 'anointed' as Aaron was, to keep the house 'walking in God's will and His path'. A question to ask ourselves: in order to favsor or please some disruptive folks in the family or society or the church– do we give in and replace God with an idol?

When the 'cat' is away

Are we the mice at play?

Application to 'self'

Do I fear people's disfavor – to let them replace God with an image? (Self-promotion)

Do I have my faith placed upon God or on my religious leaders? (self-delusion)

Do I acknowledge my sins or am I giving excuses and trying to justify myself? (Self-Pity)

Do I seek popularity? Am I trying to be a people pleaser and not a God Pleaser? (Self-Serving)

We may hold high positions, but if we have no backbone to honour the post we hold, or cannot keep our word we have a sick syndrome. (Self-Esteem)

Do I have the moral courage to stand up for what is right?

If we want popularity, we will compromise our morals and faith. (Self-Importance)

Diagnosis

'Con man' syndrome' / The Popular priest syndrome.

Con men do not accept responsibilities for personal sins and blunders of misleading and misdirecting others. Am I a People pleaser, and not a God pleaser?

2) Abraham Syndrome

Abraham was a man of great faith. By faith he left the comfort of his native city Ur to move out into the unknown wilderness, living in tents until God tells him which was to be his permanent residence. He was willing to sacrifice his own son Isaac when God asked him to do so. God called Abraham His friend and visited Abraham. None of us these days come anywhere near the stature of Abraham who has become the father of many nations.

Despite God's promise that he will have children through Sarah, Abraham 'submitted' to his wife's (nagging) wrong advice. This was the sin of presumption, as on his wife's advice he tried to give God a helping 'hand' so that God will not have trouble keeping His word! Sarah gave her 'hand-maid' as a concubine to Abraham to make a child for her. Abraham did as told by Sarah.

Bible reference

Genesis 16:2 (NIV) So she said to Abram, "The Lord has kept me from having children. Go, sleep with my maidservant; perhaps I can build a family through her." Abram agreed to what Sarai said.

Situation assessment

Later, when Hagar bore Ishmael, and God gave Isaac to Sarah as He had promised, a selfish and jealous Sarah unjustly accused Abraham about Hagar and forced Abraham to drive Hagar and Ishmael into the desert wilderness, not caring whether they would live or die!

I often wondered why Abraham allowed himself to be 'controlled' by his wife. I wonder whether it was because he sought 'political petticoat protection' by hiding behind his wife Sarah, using her as a front when they went to Egypt. Abraham repeated this mistake again later. Both times, he exposed his wife to the danger of becoming someone else's possession. Women despise their weak spouses and then dominate them. Because God had asked women to submit to their husbands, the devil does his utmost to make humanity to rebel against it. Anyway, it was Sarah who backhanded Abraham with her handmaid gained as a result of the misadventure in Egypt, for Abraham's temporary wife. This has resulted in messing up future politics of the Middle East and the whole world to this day, with countless murders and massacres shaking the entire planet.

Application to 'self'

When God calls me and treats me as a friend, do I take God for granted and allow myself to be pushed around by friends or family?

When dangers or trials come, do I take shelter behind my wife, and ask her to deal with major problems I want to avoid?

God has commissioned the man to protect, provide for, lead the family, and to love his wife. God has also asked the woman to submit to the husband. Am I rebelling against this command?

Diagnosis

Hen pecked syndrome— Matriarch dominated (Emasculated) Patriarch syndrome.

3) Absalom Syndrome

Bible reference

2 Samuel 14:25-26 (TLB) 25 Now no one in Israel was such a handsome specimen of manhood as Absalom, and no one else received such praise. 26 He cut his hair only once a year—and then only because it weighed three pounds and was too much of a load to carry around!

Self-Evaluation At The Celestial Mirror

2 Samuel 15:10-13 (TLB) 10 But while he was there, he sent spies to every part of Israel to incite rebellion against the king. "As soon as you hear the trumpets," his message read, "you will know that Absalom has been crowned in Hebron." 11 He took two hundred men from Jerusalem with him as guests, but they knew nothing of his intentions.

12— 13 A messenger soon arrived in Jerusalem to tell King David, "All Israel has joined Absalom in a conspiracy against you!"

2 Samuel 18:9-17 (TLB) 9 During the battle Absalom came upon some of David's men and as he fled on his mule, it went beneath the thick boughs of a great oak tree, and his hair caught in the branches. His mule went on, leaving him dangling in the air. 10 — — — — — — — — — — 14 "Enough of this nonsense," Joab said. Then he took three daggers and plunged them into the heart of Absalom as he dangled alive from the oak. 15 Ten of Joab's young armor-bearers then surrounded Absalom and finished him off. 16 Then Joab blew the trumpet, and his men returned from chasing the army of Israel. 17 They threw Absalom's body into a deep pit in the forest and piled a great heap of stones over it. And the army of Israel fled to their homes.

Application to 'self'
    Lust of the eyes:-The scripture warns people allowing sin to enter within them when they think that they have great beauty. Others become proud because of education, wealth, lineage or contacts. Am I one such?
    Lusts of the eye, made Absalom eye with envy his father's hard-earned throne. There are many, including politicians and paupers, who want spacious homes, good cars, and money for free spending, for which they have not laboured. Most politicians get rich by foul means. Am I one of these?
    Absalom had a grudge against his father David for not taking proper disciplinary action on Amnon his oldest son who raped his half-sister Tamar (the sister of Absalom). Do I refuse to forgive and hold on to a grudge, even a justified one?

> Absalom thought that he was the heir to
> King David and his throne.
> He groomed and pampered his glorious
> hair to heist the royal crown.
> And tried in vain to broom his father off his throne.
> His impatience to grab his heirloom.
> Cost him his head, brought on by his hair – doom

Diagnosis
   A Hairy syndrome. Covetousness was Absalom's problem

4) Adam Syndrome

Bible reference

Genesis 3:3 But of the fruit of the tree which is in the midst of the garden, God hath said, "Ye shall not eat of it, neither shall ye touch it, lest ye die".

Situation assessment

> First man was Adam to accept gastric bribery
> This is being 'followed' by bellyaching in history

When He said "do not eat that fruit", God was not depriving Adam and Eve, but was protecting them. When Eve ate it, Adam did not seek God's help to save her. Adam also did eat the forbidden fruit, deliberately. God said you will die; Adam and Eve did not obey God's warning for they did not believe God, but chose to believe Satan. They submitted their human spirits to the evil spirits.

Self-Evaluation At The Celestial Mirror

Adam and Eve died in their spirit, in their inner spirits that linked them to the Holy Spirit of God. Both Adam and Eve refused to accept responsibility; Adam put the blame on God : 'The woman you gave me made me do it!'

Application to 'self'

Am I ungrateful and taking for granted all that God has given (Self-indulgent)

Do I acknowledge my faults and sin, and repent for them or am I putting the blame on someone else? Am I trying to justify myself? (Self-righteous)

Everything in life has a choice. What is my choice? Adam resorted to rebellion and pride, which has built in 'disease and death'

When you and I are 'given' everything, do we seek out and choose 'death'?

They had God's garden Eden to live in

However, they chose to live outside in sin.

Diagnosis

Suicide syndrome; death-wish syndrome; self-destructive

5) Amnon Syndrome

Bible reference

2 Samuel 13:1-15 (TLB) 1 Prince Absalom, David's son, had a beautiful sister named Tamar. And Prince Amnon (her half-brother) fell desperately in love with her. 2 Amnon became so tormented by his love for her that he became ill. He had no way of talking to her, for the girls and young men were kept strictly apart. 3 But Amnon had a very crafty friend—his cousin Jonadab (the son of David's brother Shimeah). 4 One day Jonadab said to Amnon, "What's the trouble? Why should the son of a king look so haggard morning after morning?" So Amnon told him, "I am in love with Tamar, my half sister." 5 "Well," Jonadab said, "I'll tell you what to do. Go back to bed and pretend you are sick; when your father comes to see you, ask him to let Tamar come and prepare some food for you. Tell him you'll feel better if she feeds you."
6 So Amnon did. And when the king came to see him, Amnon asked him for this favor—that his sister Tamar be permitted to come and cook a little something for him to eat.
7 David agreed and sent word to Tamar to go to Amnon's quarters and prepare some food for him. 8 So she did and went into his bedroom so that he could watch her mix some dough; then she baked some special bread for him. 9 But when she set the serving tray before him, he refused to eat! "Everyone get out of here," he told his servants; so they all left the apartment. 10 Then he said to Tamar, "Now bring me the food again here in my bedroom and feed it to me." So Tamar took it to him. 11 But as she was standing there before him, he grabbed her and demanded, "Come to bed with me, my darling." 12 "Oh, Amnon," she cried. "Don't be foolish! Don't do this to me! You know what a serious crime it is in Israel. 13 Where could I go in my shame? And you would be called one of the greatest fools in Israel. Please, just speak to the king about it, for he will let you marry me." 14 But he wouldn't listen to her; and since he was stronger than she, he forced her. 15 Then suddenly his love turned to hate, and now he hated her more than he had loved her. "Get out of here!" he snarled at her.

Situation assessment

David's Son Amnon forcibly raped his half-sister Tamar, and then kicked her out.

David did not take any disciplinary action. Therefore, Absalom killed Amnon.

David tried to discipline Absalom. Absalom tried to dethrone David and become a king.

Absalom was 'killed' during his rebellion.

All natural secretions, expelled through natural orifices bring pleasure

Once the excretion is 'executed', the pleasure ceases and reactive rejection comes on

Amnon was 'governed' by his gonads' excretion. His mind became a toilet. Therefore, he behaved like a disposal (garbage) conduit.

Parent's sins act like genetic mutation affecting following generations. If the parent has diabetes or high blood pressure or ovarian or breast cancer it is very likely to be transmitted to the succeeding generations. King David who had wonderful qualities and in whom God was pleased had more than one wife; further, he took Bathsheba from a loyal follower of his and put Uriah her husband to death. Though David was punished for this, and repented, he glossed over Amnon's sex crime - a genetic transmission. What am I transmitting to my children and grandchildren? Do I understand that my lusts, angers, hates, bitterness, grudge holding, pride, foul mouth, envy and other bad emotions will pass down to my progeny. Is this my "will" and legacy that I leave behind?

Application to 'self'

Am I a sexual predator? Who are my targets? Do I have roving lust filled eyes?

What are my desires, and are they honourable?

Who are my friends and confidants? Friends influence their peers for good or for bad.

Do I realise that if I choose bad, immoral, evil friends or companions, they will push me into destruction. What are my present choices?

Can people trust their wives, sisters, or daughters to my care without their trust being dishonoured?

After doing something wrong against someone, do I try to make amends, or do I trash people?

Diagnosis
    Sex predator syndrome

6) Ananias & Sapphira Syndrome

Bible reference

Acts5:1-2(NASB) 1 But a certain man named Ananias, with his wife Sapphira, sold a piece of property, 2 and kept back some of the price for himself, with his wife's full knowledge, and bringing a portion of it, he laid it at the apostles' feet.

Acts 5:4-5 (TLB) 4 The property was yours to sell or not, as you wished. And after selling it, it was yours to decide how much to give. How could you do a thing like this? You weren't lying to us, but to God." 5 As soon as Ananias heard these words, he fell to the floor, dead! Everyone was terrified,

Situation assessment

> When fire and thermal power sweep
> They were looking for things to keep.

Giving is an act of love.
If selfish motives are 'woven' in, they go up in flames.
Do not look or try bait with love
Do not try to buy into or buy the Holy Spirit

Application to 'self'

When there is a revival and the Spirit of God 'falls' upon people, burning away their sin and guilt, am I trying to use the occasion for 'fund raising' or trying to elevate my 'self'?

Am I frivolously playing with the Holy Spirit - the fire of God, to warm myself instead of praying for smelting me and making me pure?

Diagnosis

If I try to salvage possessions from the 'world on fire' I will certainly be burnt!

7) Athaliah Syndrome

Bible reference

2 Kings 11:1-20 (TLB) 1 When Athaliah, the mother of King Ahaziah of Judah, learned that her son was dead, she killed all of his children, 2 except for his year-old son Joash. Joash was rescued by his Aunt Jehosheba, who was a sister of King Ahaziah (for she was a daughter of King Jehoram, Ahaziah's father). 3 She stole him away from among the rest of the king's children who were waiting to be slain and hid him and his nurse in a storeroom of the Temple. They lived there for six years while Athaliah reigned as queen. 4 In the seventh year of Queen Athaliah's reign, Jehoiada the priest summoned the officers of the palace guard and the queen's bodyguard.— — — 12 Then Jehoiada brought out the young prince and put the crown upon his head and gave him a copy of the Ten Commandments, and anointed him as king. Then everyone clapped and shouted, "Long live the king!" 13 When Athaliah heard all the noise, she ran into the Temple 14 and saw the new king standing beside the pillar, as was the custom at times of coronation, surrounded by her bodyguard and many trumpeters; and everyone was rejoicing and blowing trumpets. "Treason! Treason!" she screamed, and began to tear her clothes. 15 "Get her out of here," shouted Jehoiada to the officers of the guard. "Don't kill her here in the Temple. But kill anyone who tries to come to her rescue." 16 So they dragged her to the palace stables and

killed her there. 17 Jehoiada made a treaty between the Lord, the king, and the people, that they would be the Lord's people————
20 So everyone was happy, and the city settled back into quietness after Athaliah's death.

Application to 'self'
Do I covet to become the chief, and use any means to get there? (self-centered)
Do I demand to be the head and not the tail? (self-importance)
Though I may not kill somebody physically, do I have no qualms about killing their character so that I could get the better of them? (self-serving)
Did I have any part in aborting a child and becoming a murderer?
Am I pro-choice? Choice of what, and, for what?
Do I perform abortion or execution of defenseless bodies or people's minds?

8) Caiaphas Syndrome

Bible reference

John 11:49-53 (TLB) 49 And one of them, Caiaphas, who was High Priest that year, said, "You stupid idiots— 50 let this one man die for the people—why should the whole nation perish?" 51 This prophecy that Jesus should die for the entire nation came from Caiaphas in his position as High Priest—he didn't think of it by himself, but was inspired to say it. 52 It was a prediction that Jesus' death would not be for Israel only, but for all the children of God scattered around the world. 53 So from that time on the Jewish leaders began plotting Jesus' death.

Application to 'self'
The high priests were clever politicians even in those days. They had worked themselves into favour with their rulers - the Romans. The clergy were supposed to keep the people quite from causing any problems to the Romans. The Romans were ruthless on any insur-

rection and the priests did not want to lose their favour with the Romans.

Am I a hypocrite, hurting innocent person or persons in order promoting myself, to safeguard myself, or to curry favour with influential people?

Diagnosis
Scapegoat's finder syndrome

9) Cain Syndrome

Bible reference

Genesis 4:6-10 (KJV) 6 And the LORD said unto Cain, Why art thou wroth? and why is thy countenance fallen? 7 If thou doest well, shalt thou not be accepted? and if thou doest not well, sin lieth at the door. And unto thee shall be his desire, and thou shalt rule over him. 8 And Cain talked with Abel his brother: and it came to pass, when they were in the field, that Cain rose up against Abel his brother, and slew him. 9 And the LORD said unto Cain, Where is Abel thy brother? And he said, I know not: Am I my brother's keeper? 10 And he said, What hast thou done? the voice of thy brother's blood crieth unto me .

Situation assessment
Murderous rage overcomes when someone else does better, or is more acceptable in society. We expect full reward for a half-hearted effort.

Cain was the very first born for Adam and Eve. The parent's first fruit after eating the forbidden fruit becomes inedible, for Cain kills his younger brother!

Being a farmer – Cain probably picked up random things on plants to offer as sacrifice – not something he labored over with love cultivated, nurtured and handpicked!

Abel – brought the best of the sheep he had nurtured and cared for – to offer to God. (This offering of the lamb was the symbolization of Jesus the lamb of God coming as the sacrifice for our sins).

Therefore, God chose that which was in line with His eternal plan. Anger in Cain generated the first murder.

Application to 'self'

Does my face fall, my heart get dark, and my thoughts stormy when another and not I get favoured? Or, is it the case that not only the face, but my morals too fall.

A stranger favoured may not cause so much havoc within me as someone known to me. Do I start my own havoc to kill or maim another person's character by remarks and gossip?

When someone is 'promoted', or 'honoured', do I authoritatively whisper that they really do not deserve it and got it through dishonourable means?

Do I 'expect' full reward for a half-hearted effort? Have I ever made comments or had thoughts to hurt, maim or kill another. Murder is committed in our minds, whether they are followed up physically or not.

10) Korah Dathan (KD) Syndrome

Bible reference

Numbers 16:1-3 (TLB) 1 One day Korah (son of Izhar, grandson of Kohath, and a descendant of Levi) conspired with Dathan and Abiram (the sons of Eliab) and On (the son of Peleth), all three from the tribe of Reuben, 2 to incite a rebellion against Moses. Two hundred and fifty popular leaders, all members of the Assembly, were involved. 3 They went to Moses and Aaron and said, "We have had enough of your presumption; you are no better than anyone else; everyone in Israel has been chosen of the Lord, and he is with all of us. What right do you have to put yourselves forward, claiming that we must obey you, and acting as though you were greater than anyone else among all these people of the Lord?"

Situation assessment

These rebellious fellows could have stayed on in Egypt as slaves doing hard labour, and suffered oppression. They are like some of the present day Christians, who will avoid hardship and persecution, but claim their share if there is any prosperity.

Application to 'self'
Am I behaving as a comfortable band wagon Christian wanting to enjoy the fruits after someone else has done the major hard work of 'breaking the ice'?

Am I filled with envy and jealousy, and do I want to be recognized, as a leader, and not as a follower?

Do I want to be the lead violin player and not a second string?

Diagnosis
Rebellious and Treacherous

11) Demas Syndrome

Bible reference

Colossians 4:14 (KJV) 14 Luke, the beloved physician, and Demas, greet you.

Paul was pleased with Demas when he wrote the letter to Colossians.

2 Timothy 4:9-10 (KJV) 9 Do thy diligence to come shortly unto me:

10 For Demas hath forsaken me, having loved this present world, and is departed unto Thessalonica; Crescens to Galatia, Titus unto Dalmatia.

Demas left Paul to go after worldly pleasures he loved.

1 John 2:15-16 (KJV) 15 Love not the world, neither the things that are in the world. If any man love the world, the love of the Father is not in him. 16 For all that is in the world, the lust of the flesh, and the lust of the eyes, and the pride of life, is not of the Father, but is of the world.

Application to 'self'
   Am I a backslider?
Having been made aware of the redeeming grace of the Lord who suffered on the cross for me, and after having tasted His love, am I so ungrateful to return to my rancid stinking vomitus of worldly things?

12) Diotrephes Syndrome

Bible reference

3 John 1:9-10 (TLB) 9 I sent a brief letter to the church about this, but proud Diotrephes, who loves to push himself forward as the leader of the Christians there, does not admit my authority over him and refuses to listen to me. 10 When I come I will tell you some of the things he is doing and what wicked things he is saying about me and what insulting language he is using. He not only refuses to welcome the missionary travelers himself but tells others not to, and when they do he tries to put them out of the church.

Situation assessment
   Insubordination to Divine authority
   One person who carries the infection of sin like a little leaven in the dough can destroy the home and the church. This is specially so if it is the head of the family or the church.

Application to 'self'
   I am called to be a servant - but do I want to serve, or to be served?
   Do I fall into any of the following categories?
   Am I a single saboteur who can destroy a nation?
   Am I like the broken cog in the wheel that can wreck the wagon?
   Let me not be the one person in the marriage who causes misery and divorce
   One person in the home who ruins the family
   One person in the business causing bankruptcy
   One person in the church who shatters the harmony in the church

One person in politics making the nation stink

Let me not harbour one bad thought in the mind which can mess it up
Let me not be like the one active cancer cell in the body that can kill a person
If any Christian says 'what is in it for me?'
The beatitude or the Blessed he does not see

13) Eli Syndrome

Bible reference

1 Samuel 2:12,16,17,22,23 (NIV) 12 Eli's sons were wicked men; they had no regard for the Lord.

16 If the man said to him, "Let the fat be burned up first, and then take whatever you want," the servant would then answer, "No, hand it over now; if you don't, I'll take it by force." 17 This sin of the young men was very great in the Lord's sight, for they were treating the Lord's offering with contempt.

22 Now Eli, who was very old, heard about everything his sons were doing to all Israel and how they slept with the women who served at the entrance to the Tent of Meeting.23 So he said to them, "Why do you do such things? I hear from all the people about these wicked deeds of yours.

1 Samuel 3:11-13 (NIV)11 And the Lord said to Samuel: "See, I am about to do something in Israel that will make the ears of everyone who hears of it tingle. 12 At that time I will carry out against Eli everything I spoke against his family—from beginning to end. 13 For I told him that I would judge his family forever because of the sin he knew about; his sons made themselves contemptible, and he failed to restrain them.

Situation assessment

As an old man, Eli could not control or discipline his sons. The Bible tells that there is folly in the child, which can be removed by the rod of correction so that the child will not die. The time for correction had passed and the sons ignored the impotent old father.

Eli was an irresponsible father, and he failed to realize that as a priest, he was accountable.

Application to 'self'

As a responsible father, have I disciplined my children in God's ways, or ignored it until it is too late?

As an elder, or a pastor or a leader, am I setting a good example?

Am I praying and waiting upon God - spending my time as a good honest steward?

14) Elijah Syndrome

Bible reference

1 Kings 18:37-38 (TLB) 37 O Lord, answer me! Answer me so these people will know that you are God and that you have brought them back to yourself. 38 Then, suddenly, fire flashed down from heaven and burned up the young bull, the wood, the stones, the dust, and even evaporated all the water in the ditch!

1 Kings 18:46 (TLB) 46 and the Lord gave special strength to Elijah so that he was able to run ahead of Ahab's chariot to the entrance of the city!

1 Kings 19:2-4 (NASB77) 2 Then Jezebel sent a messenger to Elijah, saying, " So may the gods do to me and even more, if I do not make your life as the life of one of them by tomorrow about this time." 3 And he was afraid and arose and ran for his life and came to Beersheba, which belongs to Judah, and left his servant there. 4 But he himself went a day's journey into the wilderness, and came and sat down under a juniper tree; and he requested for himself that he might die, and said, "It is enough; now, O Lord, take my life, for I am not better than my fathers."

Self-Evaluation At The Celestial Mirror

Situation assessment
Spiritual success got Elijah so high
Ahead of Ahab's chariot, he did fly.

Everyone who has had a success, or gone to the mountain top, will have to come down. We are most vulnerable when we have just succeeded. Pride or satisfaction creeps in after finishing or accomplishing any major task! Once on top of the mountain it has to be only downhill. It is no wonder pride precedes a fall. Whenever there is a fall, there is self-pity unless it is replaced by repentance.

Fear and Self-pity

There was no need for Elijah to run ahead of Ahab's chariot drawn by the fastest horses in the kingdom. Elijah had brought fire from heaven, slew hundreds of Baal's priests with remarkable courage. He became so 'drained' that even the messenger from Jezebel scared him out of his wits. He hid in the wilderness and indulged in self-pity, wanting to die while running away from death. For a mighty fearless prophet who prayed down fire from heaven, and then eliminate hundreds of Baal's priests, this is a significant come down!

Application to 'self'

After every success we will face a trap. Our success brings into us a surge, which is a subtle form of pride. The Bible tells us that pride goes before every fall. Our mountain top success or experience must make us fall on our faces with humble gratitude if we want to avoid these traps.

Though my highest achievements are by no means significant, yet, how often have I gloated or bragged, making my molehills into big mountain ranges?

Have I after every trial griped in self-pity, instead of repenting and taking it to the Lord?

Do I acknowledge that it is the Lord's doing and that I had nothing to do with the victory?

15) Elisha Syndrome

Bible reference

2 Kings 2:23-24 (KJV) 23 And he went up from thence unto Bethel: and as he was going up by the way, there came forth little children out of the city, and mocked him, and said unto him, Go up, thou bald head; go up, thou bald head. 24 And he turned back, and looked on them, and cursed them in the name of the LORD. And there came forth two she bears out of the wood, and tare forty and two children of them.

Situation assessment

Elisha had witnessed Elijah carried up by chariots of fire. The mantle of Elijah fell upon Elisha. The river Jordan parted to permit Elisha to cross over as fifty prophets watched and acclaimed Elisha as their leader. Usually, we become vulnerable after a great achievement. Even a great man like Elisha could not tolerate the mocking verbal insults about his Achilles heel, namely his baldness. He had limited 'forbearance'. For, he released the bears upon his teasers.

Application to 'self'

Do I try to retaliate or get angry when any one is critical or makes fun of my appearance, behaviour, faults, successes or achievements?

When I have the power, do I use it with love as a follower of Christ should?

Do I misuse the power or position that has been loaned to me by God?

16) Esau Syndrome

Bible reference

Genesis 25:29-33 (KJV) 29 And Jacob sod pottage: and Esau came from the field, and he was faint: 30 And Esau said to Jacob, Feed me, I pray thee, with that same red pottage; for I am faint: therefore was his name called Edom. 31 And Jacob said, Sell me this day thy birthright. 32 And Esau said, Behold, I am at the point to die: and what profit shall this birthright do to me? 33 And Jacob said, Swear to me this day; and he sware unto him: and he sold his birthright unto Jacob.

Hebrews 12:16-17 (TLB) 16 Watch out that no one becomes involved in sexual sin or becomes careless about God as Esau did: he traded his rights as the oldest son for a single meal. 17 And afterwards, when he wanted those rights back again, it was too late, even though he wept bitter tears of repentance. So remember, and be careful.

Situation assessment

Esau Syndrome makes light of blessings that carry responsibilities.

Edward VIII abdicated to marry Mrs. Simpson. He had a responsibility of serving the British Empire. Nevertheless, he wanted a divorced woman more. The eldest son's duty is to stay home and mind the work of the family and help the younger ones on their way. If anyone thinks it is a chore to be avoided, and is disinclined will become a looser. The one who hates responsibility and wants to be foot loose and free is like a hunter – a chaser after what seems 'deer' to his or her heart and eyes. It will ultimately only be a chase after a mirage. There was no need for a hunter 'Esau' to provide for his family – especially when they were all herdspeople.

Esau came from the field and was "faint ". This does not go with a mighty hunter. He made light of his right and bartered away a serious responsibility for a pottage of soup. The eldest son was 'expected' to carry the responsibilities of the family, and not to go on pleasure hunting trips. Instead of tending to his cattle, he wanted game and their skins.

Isaac loved Esau – because of his taste for venison, he did not guide his son properly. Esau married two Hittite women who were 'despised' by Rebecca (mother in law problem). He is called fornicator and profane in the book of Hebrews.

Jacob swindled Esau (sibling rivalry).

Esau planned to kill Jacob his own brother!

Genesis 27:41 (TLB) So Esau hated Jacob because of what he had done to him. He said to himself, "My father will soon be gone, and then I will kill Jacob."

Application to 'self'
How do I deal with my responsibilities?
a) At home:- With wife, children, siblings; and with God in prayer.
b) At work:- Honesty
c) At socials
d) when alone: in my thoughts, desires, and my goals.
What do I chase, or hunt for? What are my recreations?
Whom do I bring into my home – Hittites?
What are my real responsibilities and am I meeting them?
Am I running around doing what I want to, rather than what I ought to?

17) Eve Syndrome

Bible reference

Genesis 3:3 (TLB) It's only the fruit from the tree at the center of the garden that we are not to eat. God says we mustn't eat it or even touch it, or we will die."

Genesis 3:6 (KJV) And when the woman saw that the tree was good for food, and that it was pleasant to the eyes, and a tree to be desired to make one wise, she took of the fruit thereof, and did eat, and gave also unto her husband with her; and he did eat.

Situation assessment

Eve was the first woman shopping for the forbidden thing, which had death attached to it.

She brought in an 'eve' (eventide) to their wonderful 'life' in Eden

> Her ears grew deaf to God's voice
> But harkened to the adder's advice
> She had asked for good advice
> Then she goes to do otherwise

Application to 'self'

Do I have a morbid fascination for any sin that is sure to hurt and kill me?

Do I think and take for granted that 'forbidden fruits' are always sweeter?

When good people and God's word give me good advice, do I despise them, ignore, or deliberately disobey them?

Do I want to be like God? Do I think that I am God because Jesus said you will be joint heirs?

God in His love may call me His child. But am I aware that I am only an animated atom and not God?

18) Felix Syndrome

Bible reference

Acts 24:25-26 (TLB) 25 And as he reasoned with them about righteousness and self-control and the judgment to come, Felix was terrified. "Go away for now," he replied, "and when I have a more convenient time, I'll call for you again 26 He also hoped that Paul would bribe him, so he sent for him from time to time and talked with him.

Situation assessment
Felix almost made it, but not quite. Some advocate receiving salvation as a 'win- win' situation, which offers people prosperity on earth with eternal life of heaven thrown in as a bonus. Felix had this expectation of wanting to get money as bribe to motivate him for seeking God.

Many have become Christians to get financial aid, or other earthly benefits. They are the rice Christians or belly Christians. The Bible emphasises genuine repentance and confession with faith as the pathway to receive God's forgiveness.

Application to 'self'
Am I seeking to connect with God in order to get material prosperity and blessings on earth as well as a mansion and a crown in heaven?

Am I such a laid back person and procrastinator, too lazy even to realise that I will not only become Mr Late, but also be too late?

Am I really willing to do God's will on earth and willing to go through the rough path following the Lord?

Repeated procrastination
Altered Felix's destination

19) Gehazi's Syndrome

Bible reference

1Kings 5:20-27 (KJV) 20 But Gehazi, the servant of Elisha the man of God, said, Behold, my master hath spared Naaman this Syrian, in not receiving at his hands that which he brought: but, as the LORD liveth, I will run after him, and take somewhat of him. 21 So Gehazi followed after Naaman. And when Naaman saw him running after him, he lighted down from the chariot to meet him, and said, "Is all well?" 22 And he said, "All is well. My master hath sent me, saying, Behold, even now there be come to me from mount Ephraim two young men of the sons of the prophets: give them, I pray thee, a talent of silver, and two changes of garments". 23 And Naaman said, "Be content, take two talents." And he urged him, and bound two talents of silver in two bags, with two changes of garments, and laid them upon two of his servants; and they bare them before him. 24 And when he came to the tower, he took them from their hand, and bestowed them in the house: and he let the men go, and they departed.25 But he went in, and stood before his master. And Elisha said unto him, "Whence comest thou, Gehazi?" And he said, "Thy servant went no whither." 26 And he said unto him, "Went not mine heart with thee, when the man turned again from his chariot to meet thee? Is it a time to receive money, and to receive garments, and oliveyards, and vineyards, and sheep, and oxen, and menservants, and maidservants? 27 The leprosy therefore of Naaman shall cleave unto thee, and unto thy seed forever." And he went out from his presence a leper as white as snow.

Application to 'self'

Gehazi had the privilege of being associated with a great man of God. He had the opportunity of becoming a man of God himself, but he chose to be an opportunist, seeking only material things for himself.

Desire for material things fosters greed. Gehazi wanted 'skin' Naaman's money and clothing to cover his skin. However, he succeeded only in getting Naaman's skin, which had a disease!

Have I been hosting 'greed' in my life?

Do I try to fleece someone else to don over my skin?

20) Haman ('Hey - man') Syndrome

Bible reference

Esther 3:1-3 (NIV) 1 After these events, King Xerxes honored Haman son of Hammedatha, the Agagite, elevating him and giving him a seat of honor higher than that of all the other nobles. 2 All the royal officials at the king's gate knelt down and paid honor to Haman, for the king had commanded this concerning him. But Mordecai would not kneel down or pay him honor. 3 Then the royal officials at the king's gate asked Mordecai, "Why do you disobey the king's command?"

Esther 3:5 (TLB) Haman was furious but decided not to lay hands on Mordecai alone, but to move against all of Mordecai's people, the Jews, and destroy all of them throughout the whole kingdom of Ahasuerus.

Application to 'self'

Do I get upset, and feel that I have not been given the recognition due to me? (This may be either real or just a perceived insult or hurt)

When I walk along, or get into an elevator and wish someone good morning and they ignore me. Does my pride get hurt, and do I get angry and plan to retaliate? (Self-esteem hurt; self-respect offended; self-importance wounded)

If I wish a friend who is talking with another friend or the boss and he does not wish me back when I greet him, do I feel humiliated?(Self-pity)

If I tell my sons or students to carry out a task and they say, they will not. Do I plan to make them pay for defying me?

In all the above examples, my pride is hurt and I get angry. I plan retaliation (self-justification)

'Hey' or 'hello' may sound okay for many, but is it perceived as "how-low, or rude" to me? The misunderstanding is in the 'degree of respect' one seems to expect during greeting, even if it is just a fleeting word or action.

Meditation and prayer

Lord let me not expect to be served, but seek to serve others

Let me not want to be honoured, but serve others and God with utmost humility.

Lord let me not allow hurts or insults or injuries to affect me and create anger within me. Let me remember that 'You', the God of Creation, allowed 'Yourself' to be humiliated, hurt and 'crucified' for my sins. Let me be your true follower.

21) Hananiah Syndrome

Bible reference

Jeremiah 28:10-11 (TLB) 10 Then Hananiah, the false prophet, took the yoke off Jeremiah's neck and broke it. 11 And Hananiah said again to the crowd that had gathered, "The Lord has promised that within two years he will release all the nations now in slavery to King Nebuchadnezzar of Babylon." At that point Jeremiah walked out.

Situation assessment
   A false prophet.
   Did Hananiah have zeal or, was it an evil spirit? Hananiah prophesied what the people wanted to hear, not what God told him to tell the people. However, in being theatrical he did a good thing. He broke the wooden yoke on Jeremiah's neck and set Jeremiah free. God makes even the evil people to bless His children without them being aware of it. God turns their evil intentions to back fire on their evil, while bringing good to His children.
   God had used Jeremiah to prophesy that He had chosen Nebuchadnezzar of Babylon as the king and his servant! In addition, he was 'instructed' to tell the Jews to submit to Nebuchadnezzar and live. God puts good people in power to bless the nation; God also elevates evil people into power as 'judgment' upon a corrupt sinful nation.

Jeremiah 27:6,7,9-11 (NASB77) 6 "And now I have given all these lands into the hand of Nebuchadnezzar king of Babylon, My servant, and I have given him also the wild animals of the field to serve him. 7 "And all the nations shall serve him, and his son, and his grandson, until the time of his own land comes; then many nations and great kings will make him their servant9 "But as for you, do not listen to your prophets, your diviners, your dreamers, your soothsayers, or your sorcerers, who speak to you, saying, 'You shall not serve the king of Babylon.' 10 "For they prophesy a lie to you, in order to remove you far from your land; and I will drive you out, and you will perish. 11 "But the nation which will bring its neck under the yoke of the king of Babylon and serve him, I will let remain on its land," declares the Lord, "and they will till it and dwell in it."

Application to 'self'

In a politically charged condition, or during war or crisis, politicians become very vociferous and exhibit severe vocal-diarrhea (Self-serving; Self-defense; Self-exaltation).

Spiritual leaders also do not hesitate to become verbal to establish or extend their influence. They , along with the scribes (book writers) and the Pharisees try to convey to the anxious public that they have a direct revelation or message from God, (surpassing the politicians!). We have seen this happening frequently during the Y2K (predictions during anticipated 2000 computer crisis). Similar predictions are still being made about war, other calamities, and the end of the world.(self-delusion; self-confidence; self-deception)

Hananiah spoke lies and his own predictions and tried to interfere with God's purpose and plan. He was cursed for lying in God's name, and died.(self-destruction)

Meditation and prayer

God do I express my personal opinions and pass them onto others as though they are Your word, pretending to be Your prophet or mouthpiece?

Lord, please forgive me and keep me from such presumptuous sin.

22) Herod Syndrome

Bible reference

Matthew 2:1-8; 12-17 (TLB) 1 Jesus was born in the town of Bethlehem, in Judea, during the reign of King Herod. At about that time some astrologers from eastern lands arrived in Jerusalem, asking, 2 "Where is the newborn King of the Jews? for we have seen his star in far-off eastern lands and have come to worship him." 3 King Herod was deeply disturbed by their question, and all Jerusalem was filled with rumors. 4 He called a meeting of the Jewish religious leaders. "Did the prophets tell us where the Messiah would be born?" he asked. 5 "Yes, in Bethlehem," they said, "for this is what the prophet Micah wrote:6 'O little town of Bethlehem, you are not just an unimportant Judean village, for a Governor shall rise from you to rule my people Israel.' " 7 Then Herod sent a private message to the astrologers, asking them to come to see him; at this meeting he found out from them the exact time when they first saw the star. Then he told them, 8 "Go to Bethlehem and search for the child. And when you find him, come back and tell me so that I can go and worship him too!"

12 But when they returned to their own land, they didn't go through Jerusalem to report to Herod, for God had warned them in a dream to go home another way. 13 After they were gone, an angel of the Lord appeared to Joseph in a dream. "Get up and flee to Egypt with the baby and his mother," the angel said, "and stay there until I tell you to return, for King Herod is going to try to kill the child." 14 That same night he left for Egypt with Mary and the baby, 15 and stayed there until King Herod's death. This fulfilled the prophet's prediction, "I have called my Son from Egypt." 16 Herod was furious when he learned that the astrologers had disobeyed him. Sending soldiers to Bethlehem, he ordered them to kill every baby boy two years old and under, both in the town and on the nearby farms, for the astrologers had told him the star first appeared to them two years before. 17 This brutal action of Herod's fulfilled the prophecy of Jeremiah.

Application to 'self'

Is Herod any different from the King or President or Judge who decides that millions of babies are to be sacrificed to their sex gods? Do they not seek to satisfy the sex craze of people who want the pleasure of sex, but not the responsibility? Do they not promote the types of sex that brings widespread infections with high mortality? Do these law makers and law keepers really care for people who look up to them?

A minister unfit to administer — am I one?

23) Herodias Syndrome (Monster-mother syndrome)

Bible reference

Matthew 14:3-12 (NIV) 3 Now Herod had arrested John and bound him and put him in prison because of Herodias, his brother Philip's wife, 4 for John had been saying to him: "It is not lawful for you to have her." 5 Herod wanted to kill John, but he was afraid of the people, because they considered him a prophet.6 On Herod's birthday the daughter of Herodias danced for them and pleased Herod so much 7 that he promised with an oath to give her whatever she asked. 8 Prompted by her mother, she said, "Give me here on a platter the head of John the Baptist." 9 The king was distressed, but because of his oaths and his dinner guests, he ordered that her request be granted 10 and had John beheaded in the prison. 11 His head was brought in on a platter and given to the girl, who carried it to her mother.

Situation assessment
   Vengeful woman scorned: John the Baptist had openly rebuked king Herod for his adulterous life with his brother's wife. Herodias was outraged and shamed. Nevertheless, she wanted to continue to be the queen. She wanted to get rid of John the Baptist before Herod got scared and returned her to his brother and her lawful husband.
   She was a monster mother, unfit to have a daughter. For, she trained her daughter to become a greater monster. The mother and her daughter Salome knew the weakness of Herod for sex. Therefore, Salome shamelessly danced a provocative dance before Herod and his court. Herod leered at her drunk, and lecherously offered her anything even up to half his kingdom probably meaning she could become the queen. She knew that Herod bit the bait and asked for the head of the saintly John on a platter. She did not merely ask that John be 'killed'. She wanted a definite proof on her hands. It defies imagination that a young girl would take and carry the bloody head and present it to her mother!

Application to 'self'

Am I a vengeful person? When someone criticizes my bad behavior, am I incapable of understanding that it is for my own good?

What kind of parent am I? Am I a good role model or, a hell-raising, demon whelping person, grooming children in such a way as to make more demons?

24) Hezekiah Syndrome

(Show-off syndrome. self-preservation)

Bible reference

Isaiah 38:1-5 (KJV) 1 In those days was Hezekiah sick unto death. And Isaiah the prophet the son of Amoz came unto him, and said unto him, Thus saith the LORD, Set thine house in order: for thou shalt die, and not live. 2 Then Hezekiah turned his face toward the wall, and prayed unto the LORD, 3 And said, Remember now, O LORD, I beseech thee, how I have walked before thee in truth and with a perfect heart, and have done that which is good in thy sight. And Hezekiah wept sore. 4 Then came the word of the LORD to Isaiah, saying, 5 Go, and say to Hezekiah, Thus saith the LORD, the God of David thy father, I have heard thy prayer, I have seen thy tears: behold, I will add unto thy days fifteen years.

Isaiah 39:2-7 (TLB) 2 Hezekiah appreciated this and took the envoys from Babylon on a tour of the palace, showing them his treasure house full of silver, gold, spices, and perfumes. He took them into his jewel rooms, too, and opened to them all his treasures—everything. 3 Then Isaiah the prophet came to the king and said, "What did they say? Where are they from?" "From far away in Babylon," Hezekiah replied. 4 "How much have they seen?" asked Isaiah. And Hezekiah replied, "I showed them everything I own, all my priceless treasures." 5 Then Isaiah said to him, "Listen to this message from the Lord Almighty: 6 "The time is coming when everything you have—all the treasures stored up by your fathers—will be carried off to Babylon. Nothing will be left. 7 And some of your own sons will become slaves, yes, eunuchs, in the palace of the king of Babylon."

Situation assessment
Prevailing personal prayer may not be for our own good in the end, if it is self-motivated. Yielding to God's will in all things is safer.
Prolonging the life of King Hezekiah in answer to his prevailing prayer did not bring a blessing, but turned out to be a curse. God used his prayer as an example to teach us about our own prayers. For, even the prayer of a righteous man, prevailing prayer can have a harmful outcome if the prayer is not in the perfect will of God. It is better to submit to God's wisdom and will. Sometimes prayers not in the will of God can be dangerous, as the devil can meet the praying person's application. Hezekiah was not bothered as long as things were going to be all right in his own life. He did not care what happened to his country after his death. He did not care about a righteous heritage. His concept of life was only temporal and selfish.

If you live for yourself and your life, brief
Generations after you may suffer strife and grief

The 15 years of grace given to Hezekiah bought him disgrace; an evil son was born who dragged the nation into gross sin.
Hezekiah made a gross error in showing off the treasures of the nation and even of the temple to the Babylonians. Later, the Babylonians invaded and plundered all the treasures, which Hezekiah had proudly displayed.

What you show off
Will one day go off

Application to 'self'
Are my prayers selfish?
Do I seek God's will in my prayer submitting and casting the 'self' away?

Am I a show off, of my possessions, children, my qualifications, or accomplishments?

25) Isaac Syndrome

Bible reference

Genesis 20:1-3 (NIV) 1 Now Abraham moved on from there into the region of the Negev and lived between Kadesh and Shur. For a while he stayed in Gerar, 2 and there Abraham said of his wife Sarah, "She is my sister." Then Abimelech king of Gerar sent for Sarah and took her.

3 But God came to Abimelech in a dream one night and said to him, "You are as good as dead because of the woman you have taken; she is a married woman."

History repeats itself! Abraham's son Isaac also came to the same place, and had the same problem. He fell into the same trap his father had.

Genesis 26:6-11 (NIV) 6 So Isaac stayed in Gerar. 7 When the men of that place asked him about his wife, he said, "She is my sister," because he was afraid to say, "She is my wife." He thought, "The men of this place might kill me on account of Rebekah, because she is beautiful." 8 When Isaac had been there a long time, Abimelech king of the Philistines looked down from a window and saw Isaac caressing his wife Rebekah. 9 So Abimelech summoned Isaac and said, "She is really your wife! Why did you say, 'She is my sister'?" Isaac answered him, "Because I thought I might lose my life on account of her." 10 Then Abimelech said, "What is this you have done to us? One of the men might well have slept with your wife, and you would have brought guilt upon us."

Situation assessment
Isaac inherited weak guts, and he put his wife in danger of being violated in the same town where a generation previously another

king - with the same name - had rebuked Abraham his father, for the same act of cowardice. For Isaac also sought 'petticoat protection' from the Philistines. Later, his wife who had lost her respect for her cowardly husband used a 'hairy-skin petty-coat' to camouflage Jacob's smooth skin and made a fool of blind Isaac into granting Jacob, the inheritance rightfully Esau's as the first-born.

Application to 'self'
God, you have commissioned me to protect and provide for my wife and the family. Please show me where I have failed. Forgive me; give me courage and grace to fulfill your command.
God forgive me for not submitting to my husband and trying to manipulate people to fulfill my own will and to have control over others.
Am I showing favoritism, setting one child against another?
Lord let me not create, aid and abet sibling rivalry

26) Jezebel Syndrome (Anti (Auntie)-Christ syndrome)

Bible reference
1 Kings 18:19 (TLB) Now bring all the people of Israel to Mount Carmel, with all 450 prophets of Baal and the 400 prophets of Asherah who are supported by Jezebel."

1 Kings 16:28,30-31 (TLB) 28 When Omri died he was buried in Samaria, and his son Ahab became king in his place.

30 But he was even more wicked than his father Omri; he was worse than any other king of Israel! 31 And as though that were not enough, he married Jezebel, the daughter of King Ethbaal of the Sidonians, and then began worshiping Baal.

1 Kings 18:4 (NIV) While Jezebel was killing off the Lord's prophets, Obadiah had taken a hundred prophets and hidden them in two caves, fifty in each, and had supplied them with food and water.

1 Kings 19:2-3 (NIV) 2 So Jezebel sent a messenger to Elijah to say, "May the gods deal with me, be it ever so severely, if by this time tomorrow I do not make your life like that of one of them." 3 Elijah was afraid and ran for his life."

1 Kings 21:5-18 (TLB) 5 "What in the world is the matter?" his wife, Jezebel, asked him. "Why aren't you eating? What has made you so upset and angry?" 6 "I asked Naboth to sell me his vineyard or to trade it, and he refused!" Ahab told her. 7 "Are you the king of Israel or not?" Jezebel demanded. "Get up and eat and don't worry about it. I'll get you Naboth's vineyard!" 8 So she wrote letters in Ahab's name, sealed them with his seal, and addressed them to the civic leaders of Jezreel, where Naboth lived. 9 In her letter she commanded: "Call the citizens together for fasting and prayer. Then summon Naboth, 10 and find two scoundrels who will accuse him of cursing God and the king. Then take him out and execute him." 11 The city fathers followed the queen's instructions.12 They called the meeting and put Naboth on trial. 13 Then two men who had no conscience accused him of cursing God and the king; and he was dragged outside the city and stoned to death. 14 The city officials then sent word to Jezebel that Naboth was dead. 15 When Jezebel heard the news, she said to Ahab, "You know the vineyard Naboth wouldn't sell you? Well, you can have it now! He's dead!" 16 So Ahab went down to the vineyard to claim it.

1 Kings 21:23-24 (NASB77) 23 "And of Jezebel also has the Lord spoken, saying, ' The dogs shall eat Jezebel in the district of Jezreel.' 24 " The one belonging to Ahab, who dies in the city, the dogs shall eat, and the one who dies in the field the birds of heaven shall eat."

Situation assessment
    Jezebel hated God and God's people. She was religious and zealous over her idols. She loved wicked ways and hosted wicked priests.

Application to 'self'

Jezebel was not only sinful; she dragged her husband along with herself into wickedness.

I may not be a king or a queen, nor wield royal power; yet do I not have sins, which are equally wicked? Is not my ego, the 'self' idol worse than the idol Baal?

Does not my laziness, and religion, without hope, faith and love, constitute the sin of 'idle' worship?

27) Jacob Syndrome

Bible reference
Genesis 27:15-19 (NIV) 15 Then Rebekah took the best clothes of Esau her older son, which she had in the house, and put them on her younger son Jacob. 16 She also covered his hands and the smooth part of his neck with the goatskins. 17 Then she handed to her son Jacob the tasty food and the bread she had made. 18 He went to his father and said, "My father." "Yes, my son," he answered. "Who is it?" 19 Jacob said to his father, "I am Esau your firstborn. I have done as you told me. Please sit up and eat some of my game so that you may give me your blessing."

Genesis 27:22-23 (TLB) 22 (Jacob goes over to his father. He feels him!) Isaac: (to himself) "The voice is Jacob's, but the hands are Esau's!" 23 The ruse convinces Isaac and he gives Jacob his blessings

Genesis32:28(NIV) Then the man said, "Your name will no longer be Jacob, but Israel, because you have struggled with God and with men and have overcome."

Situation assessment

Jacob showed favouritism to Joseph, causing his ten older sons to hate Joseph to the point of trying to kill him. Jacob had cheated his brother, his father, and was in turn cheated by his uncle Laban. One of his sons had adulterous relation with one of Jacob's wives. 'You reap what you sow'.

Jacob had a compulsive 'competitor' personality. His competition started even as he was emerging from his mother's womb. His competitive nature changed after he had his competition with the angel, in Bethel.

Jacob wanted to be successful. He believed that the end justifies the means. He tried to define his own destiny. When he gave it over to God and submitted, he became Israel.

Application to 'self'
Am I so competitive as not to hesitate using either fair or foul methods to reach my goal?
How many people have I cheated?
Am I cheating myself, and for what reason?

28) Job's friends' Syndrome

Bible reference
Job 2:11,13 (TLB) 11 When three of Job's friends heard of all the tragedy that had befallen him, they got in touch with each other and traveled from their homes to comfort and console him. Their names were Eliphaz the Temanite, Bildad the Shuhite, and Zophar the Naamathite. 13 So they sat down with him upon the ground seven days and seven nights, and none spake a word unto him: for they saw that his grief was very great.

Situation assessment
The friends started well but ended ill. For, they added coal to the fire, pain to Job's grief.
It is often better to be silent than talk foolishly. Even truth must be 'spoken' with love if love is to be conveyed. They were counselors, out of control, for they had a belief system that if a person is physically sick, it is because he or she has committed a serious sin. The disciples of Jesus also had such a belief. They asked the Lord in one instance, if the man or his parents had committed a crime, which caused a man's blindness. Jesus told them that the blindness was intended to bring glory to God, and not because of sin. He also explained to them that people who died at that time due to collapse

of a building were not worse sinners than those alive. Let God be the only judge. We are encouraged to judge ourselves, but not others.

Application to 'self'
Do I have a judgmental or critical attitude?
Do I believe that those who suffer (excepting me and those close to me) deserve what they get when it is not good?
Do I lack not only empathy, but also sympathy?

29) Jonah Syndrome

Bible reference
Jonah 1:12 (TLB) "Throw me out into the sea," he said, "and it will become calm again. For I know this terrible storm has come because of me."

Jonah 4:2 (TLB) He complained to the Lord about it: "This is exactly what I thought you'd do, Lord, when I was there in my own country and you first told me to come here. That's why I ran away to Tarshish. For I knew you were a gracious God, merciful, slow to get angry, and full of kindness; I knew how easily you could cancel your plans for destroying these people."

Jonah 4:9-11 (TLB) 9 And God said to Jonah, "Is it right for you to be angry because the plant died?" "Yes," Jonah said, "it is; it is right for me to be angry enough to die!"10 Then the Lord said, "You feel sorry for yourself when your shelter is destroyed, though you did no work to put it there, and it is, at best, short-lived.11 And why shouldn't I feel sorry for a great city like Nineveh with its 120,000 people in utter spiritual darkness and all its cattle?"

Situation assessment
Jonah hated the ruling tyrants of Nineveh, and did not even want to give them God's warning, lest they repent and get forgiven by God. So he spent his money to run away to Tarshish in the opposite direction. He was willing to be thrown into the raging sea and perish rather than go to Nineveh to offer them hope.

When God forgave, the preacher focused on success of his work, still had no forgiveness in his heart. He was not ready to accept his own hard lesson of being forgiven, saved in the sea, and provided with free transportation to Nineveh!

He did not appreciate God pardoning those in Nineveh who heeded his preaching.

Application to 'self'
Do I want to see some people suffer or die?
When my enemies prosper do I suffer self-pity and Persecution Complex?
Do I want my curses upon some people to come true?
Do I want the terrorists and the persecutors to kill themselves or to die and perish without hearing the words of hope and salvation from God?
Do I distance myself from terrorists and persecutors - physically emotionally verbally and spiritually?

30) Jonadab the Venomous Friend Syndrome;
'Perverter' syndrome

Bible reference
2 Samuel 13:1-5 (TLB) But Amnon had a very crafty friend—his cousin Jonadab (the son of David's brother Shimeah). 4 One day Jonadab said to Amnon, "What's the trouble? Why should the son of a king look so haggard morning after morning?" So Amnon told him, "I am in love with Tamar, my half sister." 5 "Well," Jonadab said, "I'll tell you what to do. Go back to bed and pretend you are sick; when your father comes to see you, ask him to let Tamar come and prepare some food for you. Tell him you'll feel better if she feeds you."

Situation assessment
When one has a friend like Jonadab, he or she does not need any murderous enemies. Being a cousin, not in the line of inheritance, he probably envied Amnon's lineage.

Rape was dealt with very seriously in those days, and there was a danger of a rapist being stoned to death. He hatched out a plan to enable Amnon to rape his half-sister Tamar. To say the least, Jonadab was wicked and planned his friend's eventual death.

Application to 'self'
What sort of a friend am I?
Do I lead a friend who trusts me into sin, which has a penalty of hell and eternal separation from God?
Do I get my friend into danger (physical, emotional or spiritual) knowingly, deliberately?

31) Joseph Syndrome "Jo Soap"

Bible reference

Genesis 37:4-10 (TLB) 4 His brothers of course noticed their father's partiality, and consequently hated Joseph; they couldn't say a kind word to him.

5 One night Joseph had a dream and promptly reported the details to his brothers, causing even deeper hatred. 6 "Listen to this," he proudly announced. 7 "We were out in the field binding sheaves, and my sheaf stood up, and your sheaves all gathered around it and bowed low before it!" 8 "So you want to be our king, do you?" his brothers derided. And they hated him both for the dream and for his cocky attitude. 9 Then he had another dream and told it to his brothers. "Listen to my latest dream," he boasted. "The sun, moon, and eleven stars bowed low before me!"

Situation assessment
When Joseph was young and not mature, he was handicapped because of his father Jacob's partiality.
Speaking prematurely!
Sharing his prophetic dreams with his angry brothers nearly got him killed.

There is a time to talk and a time to keep quiet. Joseph learnt this hard lesson the hard way.

Laundry problem:- He laundered his dreams with his brothers and parents. His dreams were not his brothers'. Therefore, they dreamed up a nightmare for Joseph.

When we speak out our dreams and ambitions and visions to people who are unable to or cannot share in them, we will only create opponents or enemies.

We have to behave as though we were secret service agents on a top-secret mission, remain silent and anonymous, until God wants us to come out in the open with His message and action.

Application to 'self'
Am I speaking out of turn?
Do I need to learn to hold my tongue, but keep the revelation in my heart (as did Mary the mother of Jesus)? Do I act like a favoured son by flaunting my religion upon my siblings and others at every chance, seeking to intimidate them?

Do I flaunt and show off the gifts and talents God has given to me to be used in His service for His glory? Joseph showed off his multi-colored coat given exclusively to him by his doting father adding to the anger in his siblings - who saw only 'red' !

32) Judas Iscariot Syndrome

Bible reference

Matthew 27:3 (NIV) When Judas, who had betrayed him, saw that Jesus was condemned, he was seized with remorse and returned the thirty silver coins to the chief priests and the elders.

2 Corinthians 7:10 (NIV) Godly sorrow brings repentance that leads to salvation and leaves no regret, but worldly sorrow brings death.

Situation assessment
Repentance = sorrow for sins + hope on God's mercy + faith on Jesus to forgive.

Remorse = grief, loss of hope in God's mercy with a sense of doom, self-condemnation (desperate, with no hope or faith) internal rebellion, depression; diabolic control of the mind producing death wish with suicidal and homicidal thoughts and a 'be damned attitude'.

Repentance follows conviction that a person is a dreadful sinner in need of a Saviour. This blessing upon people is by the mercy of the Holy Spirit of God. At this time, the Holy Spirit points the person to the Cross and to Jesus who has paid for the person's sins. He also helps one to trust Jesus and ask for forgiveness, to clean the inside and come in and be the Lord and Master. This results in receiving the gift of salvation through faith in Jesus, Son of God.

Sorrow, one without hope of being 'forgiven', is due to lack of faith in the loving promises of God. This hopelessness is called remorse, leading to death - not repentance which leads to salvation.

Judas had a physically close association with Jesus. He was received into the inner circle of disciples, given the power to heal the sick and had the opportunity to listen to the Sermon on the Mount and the many parables. He wanted to be in charge of the purse, and sadly the purse pursued him to make him forsake his Master and friend.

Application to 'self'
Do I have hope in God and His mercy?
Do I have faith to trust the Lord during my sickness and tribulation?
Am I seeking and trusting in money or the Master of my life?

33) King David's Syndrome

Bible reference

2 Samuel 12:1-13 (NIV) 1 The LORD sent Nathan to David. When he came to him, he said, "There were two men in a certain town, one rich and the other poor. 2 The rich man had a very large number of sheep and cattle, 3 but the poor man had nothing except one little ewe lamb he had bought. He raised it, and it grew up with him and

his children. It shared his food, drank from his cup and even slept in his arms. It was like a daughter to him. 4 "Now a traveler came to the rich man, but the rich man refrained from taking one of his own sheep or cattle to prepare a meal for the traveler who had come to him. Instead, he took the ewe lamb that belonged to the poor man and prepared it for the one who had come to him." 5 David burned with anger against the man and said to Nathan, "As surely as the LORD lives, the man who did this deserves to die! 6 He must pay for that lamb four times over, because he did such a thing and had no pity." 7 Then Nathan said to David, "You are the man! This is what the LORD, the God of Israel, says: 'I anointed you king over Israel, and I delivered you from the hand of Saul.

8 I gave your master's house to you, and your master's wives into your arms. I gave you the house of Israel and Judah. And if all this had been too little, I would have given you even more.

9 Why did you despise the word of the LORD by doing what is evil in his eyes? You struck down Uriah the Hittite with the sword and took his wife to be your own. You killed him with the sword of the Ammonites. 10 Now, therefore, the sword will never depart from your house, because you despised me and took the wife of Uriah the Hittite to be your own.'

Situation assessment

It took someone else to point out to King David that what he did in secret was wrong and not a secret any more. By trying to hide the evils we do from the sight of others, we end up hiding it only from our own selves. It is called a "denial" phenomenon. God's mirror acts like a good mirror and a telescope, no one can escape its sights and exposure.

Application to 'self'

Do not cover your eyes with a patch while looking into a mirror. David tried to, but got hurt. Self-indulgence leads to other self-trap.

34) Laban Syndrome

Bible reference

Genesis 24:29-55 (NIV) 29 Now Rebekah had a brother named Laban, and he hurried out to the man at the spring. 30 As soon as he had seen the nose ring, and the bracelets on his sister's arms, and had heard Rebekah tell what the man said to her, he went out to the man and found him standing by the camels near the spring. 31 "Come, you who are blessed by the Lord," he said. "Why are you standing out here? I have prepared the house and a place for the camels

53 Then the servant brought out gold and silver jewelry and articles of clothing and gave them to Rebekah; he also gave costly gifts to her brother and to her mother

Genesis 31:5-7 (NASB77) 5 and said to them, " I see your father's attitude, that it is not friendly toward me as formerly, but the God of my father has been with me. 6 "And you know that I have served your father with all my strength. 7 "Yet your father has cheated me and changed my wages ten times; however, God did not allow him to hurt me.

Application to 'self'
    Do I subscribe to the policy of 'lying to get someone married is not a sin'?
    Do I cut corners and more, in the wages of people working for me?
    This can be summarized as "con artist conned syndrome"

35) Laodicea Church Syndrome

Bible reference

Revelation 3:14-20 (TLB) 14 "Write this letter to the leader of the church in Laodicea: "This message is from the one who stands firm, the faithful and true Witness [of all that is or was or evermore shall be], the primeval source of God's creation:15 "I know you well—you are neither hot nor cold; I wish you were one or the other! 16 But since you are merely lukewarm, I will spit you out of my mouth! 17 "You say, 'I am rich, with everything I want; I don't need a thing!' And you don't realize that spiritually you are wretched and miserable and poor and blind and naked. 18 "My advice to you is to buy pure gold from me, gold purified by fire—only then will you truly be rich. And to purchase from me white garments, clean and pure, so you won't be naked and ashamed; and to get medicine from me to heal your eyes and give you back your sight. 19 I continually discipline and punish everyone I love; so I must punish you unless you turn from your indifference and become enthusiastic about the things of God. 20 "Look! I have been standing at the door, and I am constantly knocking. If anyone hears me calling him and opens the door, I will come in and fellowship with him and he with me.

Application to 'self'

Have I chosen to be in a warm cosy comfort zone? Comfortable religion, not passionately hot for doing God's will, nor too cold to be obvious to the onlookers as being one dead cold.

Do I trust in my salary, or the savings in the bank account, or on God to support me?

Do I have music or TV on the whole time, creating a din so that I cannot hear the Lord's soft knocking at the heart?

Double minded is to double cross

36) Lot Syndrome

Bible reference

Genesis 13:9 (TLB) "I'll tell you what we'll do. Take your choice of any section of the land you want, and we will separate. If you want that part over there to the east, then I'll stay here in the western section. Or, if you want the west, then I'll go over there to the east."

Lot was selfish, chose what he thought was best for him-self, when his more needy friend and mentor offered him the first choice.

His choice turned to ashes in more than one way (as Sodom and Gomorrah did).

Genesis 13:10 (TLB) Lot took a long look at the fertile plains of the Jordan River, well watered everywhere (this was before Jehovah destroyed Sodom and Gomorrah); the whole section was like the Garden of Eden, or like the beautiful countryside around Zoar in Egypt.

Trouble starts with a willful, wrong choice.

Genesis 13:12-13 (KJV) 12 Abram dwelled in the land of Canaan, and Lot dwelled in the cities of the plain, and pitched his tent toward Sodom. 13 But the men of Sodom were wicked and sinners before the LORD exceedingly.

Where do you pitch your tent? Is it close to the place of peril and evil?
Lot exposes his family – wife and children to evil.

Genesis 13:18 (NIV) So Abram moved his tents and went to live near the great trees of Mamre at Hebron, where he built an altar to the Lord.

(In contrast, Abraham went near woods and built an 'altar' for God and pitched his tents there – near the place of worship.)

Genesis 14:12 (NIV) They also carried off Abram's nephew Lot and his possessions, since he was living in Sodom.

'Lot's lot' with Sodom:
God shows that power of Kings cannot deliver Lot

Genesis 14:15-16 (NIV) 15 During the night Abram divided his men to attack them and he routed them, pursuing them as far as Hobah, north of Damascus. 16 He recovered all the goods and brought back his relative Lot and his possessions, together with the women and the other people.

Through a small group of god fearing Abraham and his men, God delivered Lot and the kings.

Genesis 14:23-24 (TLB) 21 The king of Sodom told him, "Just give me back my people who were captured; keep for yourself the booty stolen from my city." . . . . . . 24 All I'll accept is what these young men of mine have eaten; but give a share of the loot to Aner, Eshcol, and Mamre, my allies." that I will not take so much as a single thread from you, lest you say, 'Abram is rich because of what I gave him!'
Do not receive gifts from evil people.

Genesis 14:20-21 (TLB) and blessed be God, who has delivered your enemies over to you. Then Abram gave Melchizedek a tenth of all the loot.

Abraham gives tithes to Melchisedek, the priest. He also shared food and fellowship –with him, which should have been a lesson to Lot. However, this did not register - resulting in the consequences of Lot's life in Sodom.

Genesis 19:1-8 (TLB) 1 That evening the two angels came to the entrance of the city of Sodom, and Lot was sitting there as they arrived. When he saw them he stood up to meet them, and welcomed them. 2 "Sirs," he said, "come to my home as my guests for the night; you can get up as early as you like and be on your way again." "Oh, no thanks," they said, "we'll just stretch out here along the street." 3 But he was very urgent, until at last they went home with him, and he set a great feast before them, complete with freshly baked unleavened bread. After the meal,

4 as they were preparing to retire for the night, the men of the city—yes, Sodomites, young and old from all over the city—surrounded the house 5 and shouted to Lot, "Bring out those men to us

so we can rape them." 6 Lot stepped outside to talk to them, shutting the door behind him.

7 "Please, fellows," he begged, "don't do such a wicked thing. 8 Look—I have two virgin daughters, and I'll surrender them to you to do with as you wish. But leave these men alone, for they are under my protection."

Lot's bargains are bad – he knows about hospitality, but is selfish. He offers his daughters (not himself) to the Sodomites. His value of morality and his family was terribly flawed.

Genesis 19:14 (KJV) And Lot went out, and spake unto his sons in law, which married his daughters, and said, Up, get you out of this place; for the LORD will destroy this city. But he seemed as one that mocked unto his sons in law.

Genesis 19:26 (TLB) But Lot's wife looked back as she was following along behind him and became a pillar of salt.

Lot could not save his wife even when they were out of Sodom

Genesis 19:18-19 (TLB) 18 "Oh no, sirs, please," Lot begged, 19 "since you've been so kind to me and saved my life, and you've granted me such mercy, let me flee to that little village over there instead of into the mountains, for I fear disaster in the mountain.

Lot does not want to go to the hills but to a town – for a comfortable location. Then he was afraid whether there will be problem there like in Sodom and went to the hill - this time without the protection and cover of God's angels, inviting more trouble.

Genesis 19:31-36 (TLB) 31 One day the older girl said to her sister, "There isn't a man anywhere in this entire area that our father would let us marry. And our father will soon be too old for having children. 32 Come, let's fill him with wine and then we will sleep with him, so that our clan will not come to an end." 33 So they got him drunk that night, and the older girl went in and had sexual intercourse with her father; but he was unaware of her lying down or getting up again.

34 The next morning she said to her younger sister, "I slept with my father last night. Let's fill him with wine again tonight, and you go in and lie with him, so that our family line will continue." 35 So they got him drunk again that night, and the younger girl went in and lay with him, and, as before, he didn't know that anyone was there. 36 And so it was that both girls became pregnant from their father.

Lot's daughters had not been 'taught', or learnt any 'moral' standards as they grew up in the evil immoral city Sodom.

Yes, Lot has a 'lot' of lessons to offer for our thoughts, a whole lot of thoughts!

Application to 'self'

When a benefactor offers me two options from his own personal resources, would I choose what will cost him more?

If I have to decide between two job offers, and standards are the same, would I choose one in a glamorous city (self-centered choice), or in a stable God honouring smaller city?

37) The Lying Prophet Syndrome

Bible reference

1 Kings 13:11-24 (TLB)11 As it happened, there was an old prophet living in Bethel, and his sons went home and told him what the prophet from Judah had done and what he had said to the king.12 "Which way did he go?" the old prophet asked. So they told him. 13 "Quick, saddle the donkey," the old man said. And when they had saddled the donkey for him,14 he rode after the prophet and found him sitting under an oak tree. "Are you the prophet who came from Judah?" he asked him. "Yes," he replied, "I am." 15 Then the old man said to the prophet, "Come home with me and eat." 16 "No," he replied, "I can't; for I am not allowed to eat anything or to drink any water at Bethel. 17 The Lord strictly warned me against it; and he also told me not to return home by the same road I came on." 18

But the old man said, "I am a prophet too, just as you are; and an angel gave me a message from the Lord. I am to take you home with me and give you food and water." But the old man was lying to him. 19 So they went back together, and the prophet ate some food and drank some water at the old man's home. 20 Then, suddenly, while they were sitting at the table, a message from the Lord came to the old man, 21 and he shouted at the prophet from Judah, "The Lord says that because you have been disobedient to his clear command 22 and have come here, and have eaten and drunk water in the place he told you not to, therefore your body shall not be buried in the grave of your fathers." 23 After finishing the meal, the old man saddled the prophet's donkey, 24 and the prophet started off again. But as he was traveling along, a lion came out and killed him. His body lay there on the road, with the donkey and the lion standing beside it.

Situation assessment

The end result: death of the prophet from Judah, for a lion killed him. This was the reason God had told him not to eat or delay and to take a different, safer route. The so-called prophet from Bethel wanted the courageous prophet from Judah who had faced the king and came out triumphant, to come to his house so that he can brag about his own influence and importance.. Such people want to be in the lime light (they don't have their own) , use any means to trap people so that others could believe that these spongers have connection and influence. They exploit this to their own advantage. These dangerous people belong to all walks of life and constantly seek out gullible, important, or successful persons. These predators will proclaim relationship, or close alliance with any person of importance or success, with an idea of exploiting the important person for their own profit. They will not think twice about destroying or ditching the one through whom they acquired their benefits, once their purpose is accomplished. They are like parasites, which mercilessly suck out their hosts' blood and life. These predators try to get into a bandwagon already paid for, or pulled by somebody else. Our self-evaluation must help us to see if we belong to this predator/parasitic group.

The following are the clues
That brings into your life, blues

Application to 'self'

Am I trying to get close to influential people with an ulterior motive of getting personal benefits?

Do I tell people that God asked them to do something, and is using me as His messenger?

Do I lie in the name of God?

38) Martha Syndrome

Bible reference

Luke 10:39-42 (NIV) 39 She had a sister called Mary, who sat at the Lord's feet listening to what he said. 40 But Martha was distracted by all the preparations that had to be made. She came to him and asked, "Lord, don't you care that my sister has left me to do the work by myself? Tell her to help me!" 41 "Martha, Martha," the Lord answered, "you are worried and upset about many things, 42 but only one thing is needed. Mary has chosen what is better, and it will not be taken away from her."

Situation assessment

Martha placed 'Body needs' before 'Soul needs'. Many women believe that a way to a man's heart is through the stomach. Gastric pathways to the heart are essentially equal to gastric bribery.

It was a choice for Martha and Mary to entertain people and spend time doing so – or make use of the brief visits they had from Jesus. Hospitality includes feeding the guests. Nevertheless, feeding the guests forms only a small part of hospitality. It is only hotels and eating-places that offer food of different sorts for different tastes.

Jesus would have preferred not to be entertained – but to have their ears and hearts and feed on His word and drink the Life giving living water. Martha mistook Mary's choice of staying at His feet as a poor one. She thought and judged her sister as lazy and irresponsible. It was only when she complained to Jesus to correct Mary, that Jesus told her that He preferred Mary's action to her own (Martha's).

Application to 'self'

Do I spend more time and energy in entertaining visitors and others, and give only a fraction of the time in prayer – on any average day?

Who is my regular or frequent guest?

Do I choose to entertain Jesus, or my friends, family, people with power or position, or the rich?

How do I entertain people? Do I ply them with food, soda, whisky and beer? Or is it with a game of cards, chitchat, or porno-movie?

Do I offer to have Bible study or prayer as often as I offer refreshments and food?

39) Mordecai Syndrome (provoker syndrome)

Bible reference

Esther 3:3 (TLB) "Why are you disobeying the king's commandment?" the others demanded day after day, but he still refused. Finally they spoke to Haman about it to see whether Mordecai could get away with it because of his being a Jew, which was the excuse he had given them.

Situation assessment

Some people invite trouble by deliberately baiting, insulting and irritating others. Being an obstacle or setting up another person to make mistakes is criminal. The ones with the syndrome have a bloated feeling of becoming 'selfless' martyrs by provoking someone else to sin.

When someone says no, or wants to be 'excused', I must not insist that they do what I think they should do. I may think that I am a true Christian and the other is not, therefore not worthy of my respect. Mordecai was a Jew and worshipped the true God. He was not expected to worship Haman - but commanded to show due respect by the king's order. Mordecai had no business to be at the gate through which Haman was coming to the palace, every day. Mordecai's act was deliberate, belligerent defiance, and an insult to Haman. With such behaviour, I become an obstacle for those seeking God. My spirituality should not be 'aimed' to provoke others - unless God wants me to confront them with the gospel.

Application to 'self'
Do I think that I come from a big family, have royal blood, smarter or have better looks than someone else in my 'sights'?
Do I derive pleasure making another angry?
Do I make jokes on others in order to humiliate them?

40) Nicodemus Syndrome

Bible reference

John 3:1-8 (TLB) 1 After dark one night a Jewish religious leader named Nicodemus, a member of the sect of the Pharisees, 2 came for an interview with Jesus. "Sir," he said, "we all know that God has sent you to teach us. Your miracles are proof enough of this."

Jesus replied, "With all the earnestness I possess I tell you this: Unless you are born again, you can never get into the Kingdom of God." 4 "Born again!" exclaimed Nicodemus. "What do you mean? How can an old man go back into his mother's womb and be born again?" 5 Jesus replied, "What I am telling you so earnestly is this: Unless one is born of water and the Spirit, he cannot enter the Kingdom of God. 6 Men can only reproduce human life, but the Holy Spirit gives new life from heaven; 7 so don't be surprised at my statement that you must be born again! 8 Just as you can hear the wind but can't tell where it comes from or where it will go next, so it is with the Spirit. We do not know on whom he will next bestow this life from heaven."

Application to 'self'
   Am I ashamed of God?
   Am I ashamed to declare that I belong to God?
   Am I afraid to proclaim God?
   There is a very limited place for a secret disciple during massive persecution.

Seekers may like secrecy,
   but disciples need to follow and proclaim openly.

41) Pharaoh Syndrome

Bible reference

Exodus 1:15 (TLB) Then Pharaoh, the king of Egypt, instructed the Hebrew midwives (their names were Shiphrah and Puah) to kill all Hebrew boys as soon as they were born, but to let the girls live.

Exodus 6:1 (TLB) "Now you will see what I shall do to Pharaoh," the Lord told Moses. "For he must be forced to let my people go; he will not only let them go, but will drive them out of his land!

Self-Evaluation At The Celestial Mirror

Exodus 9:34 (KJV) And when Pharaoh saw that the rain and the hail and the thunders were ceased, he sinned yet more, and hardened his heart, he and his servants.

Pharaoh matched his might and majesty against God almighty and made light of the warnings, plagues and advice. Pharaoh had to be 'judged' for ordering male Hebrew children to be killed at birth. He was like a monkey with its hand in the peanut jar - would not let go and was caught.

Exodus 12:29 (NASB77) Now it came about at midnight that the Lord struck all the first-born in the land of Egypt, from the first-born of Pharaoh who sat on his throne to the first-born of the captive who was in the dungeon, and all the first-born of cattle.

The judgment was 'The first-borns of Egypt would die'.

Exodus 14:9-30 (TLB) 9 Pharaoh's entire cavalry—horses, chariots, and charioteers—was used in the chase; and the Egyptian army overtook the people of Israel — — —. 10 As the Egyptian army approached, the people of Israel saw them far in the distance, speeding after them, and they were terribly frightened and cried out to the Lord to help them. 11 — — — — — — — — — — —." 13 But Moses told the people, "Don't be afraid. Just stand where you are and watch, and you will see the wonderful way the Lord will rescue you today. The Egyptians you are looking at—you will never see them again. 14 The Lord will fight for you, and you won't need to lift a finger!" 15 — — — — — — — — — — — the sea will open up a path before you, and all the people of Israel shall walk through on dry ground! — — — — — — — 17 — — — — — — — 22 So the people of Israel walked through the sea on dry ground! 23 Then the Egyptians followed them between the walls of water along the bottom of the sea—all of Pharaoh's horses, chariots, and horsemen. 27 and the sea returned to normal beneath the morning light. The Egyptians tried to flee, but the Lord drowned them in the sea. 28 The water covered the path and the chariots and horsemen. And of all the army of Pharaoh that chased after Israel through the sea, not one remained alive.

Application to 'self'

This Pharaoh must have had a historical knowledge about how God had used Joseph to save Egypt and its people from the severe seven year famine. Do I forget how God helped my parents and grandparents or fore fathers to bring me into the world now?

The Pharaoh was presuming that the Israelites who believed in God Jehovah might create a problem for his self-assumed divinity, which was accepted by the local Egyptians. He tried using the midwives to kill the Hebrew babies while they were being delivered. When it did not work out, he made a rule that all male new-borns 'must' be put to death.

God has implanted laws into nature, which when broken, will hurt the individual who breaks the law, as the "action that goes around will come around like a boomerang". Anyone who tries to jump off a height without protective contraptions will land in a hospital - if not a morgue. If we do not repent, but persist in our self-esteem, self-importance or self-elevation, we too will come down hard, like Pharoah.

When trials come upon me, do I try to overcome them by my own strength, or by getting help from my army of political friends or goondas? Or, do I seek God's mercy and wisdom?

On the other hand, do I play the fool with God by saying "help me this time, and next time I will obey", over and over like a cracked record like Pharaoh did?

42) Pharisee Syndrome (Far-is-he syndrome)

Bible reference

Matthew 23:25-28 (NIV) 25 "Woe to you, teachers of the law and Pharisees, you hypocrites! You clean the outside of the cup and dish, but inside they are full of greed and self-indulgence. 26 Blind Pharisee! First clean the inside of the cup and dish, and then the outside also will be clean. 27 "Woe to you, teachers of the law and Pharisees, you hypocrites! You are like whitewashed tombs, which look beautiful on the outside but on the inside are full of dead men's bones and everything unclean. 28 In the same way, on the outside you appear to people as righteous but on the inside you are full of hypocrisy and wickedness.

Situation assessment

> Does your life have only an outer show
> With no Godly goodness of inner glow

Sepulchres above the ground have marble stones with exquisite carvings and gold letterings. However, hidden underneath, lie death, decay, rottenness, and dead bones.

Application to 'self'
Am I thrusting into other's throats or minds 'my' opinions, ideas, and rules?
Am I self-righteous - arrogant, proud, rigid, and 'unwilling' to learn or change?
Am I 'un-teachable', therefore unreachable?
Do I have an attitude that I am a good person - usually right and seldom wrong? Am I the 'never tolerate any nonsense' type, tough and confident and believe that "I can do all things if I put my mind to it"?
Am I a camouflaged death container (white coated sepulchre)?

43) Pilate Syndrome

Bible reference

Matthew 27:24 (NIV) When Pilate saw that he was getting nowhere, but that instead uproar was starting, he took water and washed his hands in front of the crowd. "I am innocent of this man's blood," he said. "It is your responsibility!"

Situation assessment
Pilate tried to be a people pleaser, not a God pleaser. He had no conscience. He had Jesus scourged to appease a bloodthirsty crowd. The blood lust caused him to hand Jesus over to Crucifixion. He

tried 'tricks' to keep his conscience clear and clean, which did not work; these in fact never work when any one tries to please people, or placate politicians.

Application to 'self'
   Do I wash my hands off after handling a situation badly?
   Do I refuse to accept responsibility for my bad actions?
   Does self interest distort my better judgment?

44) Prodigal Son Syndrome

Bible reference

Luke 15:11-24 (NIV) 11 Jesus continued: "There was a man who had two sons 12 The younger one said to his father, 'Father, give me my share of the estate.' So he divided his property between them. 13 "Not long after that, the younger son got together all he had, set off for a distant country and there squandered his wealth in wild living. 14 After he had spent everything, there was a severe famine in that whole country, and he began to be in need. 15 So he went and hired himself out to a citizen of that country, who sent him to his fields to feed pigs. 16 He longed to fill his stomach with the pods that the pigs were eating, but no one gave him anything. 17 "When he came to his senses, he said, 'How many of my father's hired men have food to spare, and here I am starving to death!

8 I will set out and go back to my father and say to him: Father, I have sinned against heaven and against you. 19 I am no longer worthy to be called your son; make me like one of your hired men.' 20 So he got up and went to his father. "But while he was still a long way off, his father saw him and was filled with compassion for him; he ran to his son, threw his arms around him and kissed him. 21 "The son said to him, 'Father, I have sinned against heaven and against you. I am no longer worthy to be called your son.' 22 "But the father said to his servants, 'Quick! Bring the best robe and put it on him. Put a ring on his finger and sandals on his feet. 23 Bring the fattened calf and kill it. Let's have a feast and celebrate. 24 For this son of mine was dead and is alive again; he was lost and is found.' So they began to celebrate.

Situation assessment

He wandered and squandered to find he was lost and damned. He was outside of his father's house. The prodigal son did not want to stay and help his father. He was selfish and wanted to get his hands on his father's money and live his own life. The father worked for the money, and all that the son wants is half of it, to indulge in selfish pleasures.

This attitude will make you banish yourself from your home, make you wander with nowhere to go. You will squander your wealth and lose your health, eventually competing for food with the likes of swine (pigs). Finally it was because of swine that he learnt the lesson that he was a prodigal son, a lost creature and that it would be better for him to return to his father's house.

> Be careful how you arrange any sentence
> Lest, the sequence brings a bad sentence

You and I become prodigals when we say "Give For Me".
We need to rectify it by proper alignment of the words," For Give Me", addressing God. We should then be willing to be of use in God's family. Whoever leaves God to pursue selfish desires will risk losing not only their health and wealth (medical bills) on earth but

also the safety and security of their eternal home. Association with swine and a longing to feed on swine food, will break their pride.

Application to 'self'
  At what stage of the Prodigal's life, am I in?
  Do I want my Father's money to go away and enjoy selfishly, or be willing to stay and help and be a comfort to the Father?
  Do I get away from home to escape my commitments and responsibilities?

45) Rebecca Syndrome

Bible reference

Genesis 25:28 (TLB) Isaac's favorite was Esau, because of the venison he brought home, and Rebekah's favorite was Jacob.

Genesis 27:6-13 (KJV) 6 And Rebekah spake unto Jacob her son, saying, Behold, I heard thy father speak unto Esau thy brother, saying,7 Bring me venison, and make me savoury meat, that I may eat, and bless thee before the LORD before my death. 8 Now therefore, my son, obey my voice according to that which I command thee. 9 Go now to the flock, and fetch me from thence two good kids of the goats; and I will make them savoury meat for thy father, such as he loveth:

10 And thou shalt bring it to thy father, that he may eat, and that he may bless thee before his death. 11 And Jacob said to Rebekah his mother, Behold, Esau my brother is a hairy man, and I am a smooth man: 12 My father peradventure will feel me, and I shall seem to him as a deceiver; and I shall bring a curse upon me, and not a blessing. 13 And his mother said unto him, Upon me be thy curse, my son: only obey my voice, and go fetch me them.

Genesis 27:42-46 (NIV) 42 When Rebekah was told what her older son Esau had said, she sent for her younger son Jacob and said to him, "Your brother Esau is consoling himself with the thought of killing you. 43 Now then, my son, do what I say: Flee at once to my brother Laban in Haran. 44 Stay with him for a while until your brother's fury subsides. 45 When your brother is no longer angry with you and forgets what you did to him, I'll send word for you to come back from there. Why should I lose both of you in one day?" 46 Then Rebekah said to Isaac, "I'm disgusted with living because of these Hittite women. If Jacob takes a wife from among the women of this land, from Hittite women like these, my life will not be worth living."

Situation assessment

She was a rebellious, passive aggressive wife, and not submissive. God showed her during her pregnancy that her second will be the leader of the two. She should have prayed for the first-born more, so that he too would be acceptable to God. Instead, she favored the second. She knew who was going to be the boss, so backed the winner.It is sad that some mothers ignore or ill-treat the mentally incompetent child and favor the more beautiful or talented child.

She favoured Jacob over Esau. She taught Jacob how to make a fool of his father. She accepted full responsibility for using her son to cheat and hoodwink a blind old man, the impotent father. At the same time, she deprived her non-favourite son Esau.When she found her husband favored the first born, she chose the second for herself (favoritism in family!). Isaac had enough meat (vast herds of cattle) but he liked 'game' meat and encouraged his first born to go a-hunting.

This fostered lasting jealousy and enmity between the brothers and their progeny. She brought a curse upon her (for she died before Jacob returned from exile), and upon her own grandchildren who are alienated to this day in the Middle East! Her husband, who she thought was dying, outlived her.

Application to 'self'

Do I favour one child or grandchild or one sibling over the other?

Does my legacy leave peace or conflict for the following generations?

46) Sadducee Syndrome (Sad u see syndrome)

Bible reference

Matthew 3:7-9 (NIV) 7 But when he saw many of the Pharisees and Sadducees coming to where he was baptizing, he said to them: "You brood of vipers! Who warned you to flee from the coming wrath? 8 Produce fruit in keeping with repentance.

Matthew 16:11-12 (NIV) 11 How is it you don't understand that I was not talking to you about bread? But be on your guard against the yeast of the Pharisees and Sadducees." 12 Then they understood that he was not telling them to guard against the yeast used in bread, but against the teaching of the Pharisees and Sadducees.

Matthew 22:23 (NIV) 23 That same day the Sadducees, who say there is no resurrection, came to him with a question.

Acts 23:8 (NIV) 8 (The Sadducees say that there is no resurrection, and that there are neither angels nor spirits, but the Pharisees acknowledge them all.)

Situation assessment

The Sadducee has no real hope in God. When there is no hope of resurrection and no life beyond, it is no wonder that he or she is 'sad - u – see'

Life is not worth living if there is no hope. Many commit suicide when they lose all hope. Patients go into a deep shock when told that they have a terminal illness like cancer or a bad heart, or bad lung, or bad kidney or a bad liver disease. People without hope need to keep their mouth shut, not teach or preach, so they do not inflict or infect others who seek to invest into the future. We are unconsciously teaching others (especially our children) who look up to us silently. If we live having no hope for the future, alas, our children may also believe that there is no future life. However, God seeks even people in such situations and offers restoration and installation of hope.

> If there is a big sin in your soul
> Your 'hope' through it can fall

The Bible is full of hope for even the hopeless. Let us look at some examples:

Hope is strength

(Job 6:1) Hope perishes when you forget God
Job 8:13 (KJV) So are the paths of all that forget God; and the hypocrite's hope shall perish:

Job 11:18 (KJV) And thou shalt be secure, because there is hope; yea, thou shalt dig about thee, and thou shalt take thy rest in safety.

Hope makes you secure - you 'dig in'.

Job 27:8 (NIV) For what hope has the godless when he is cut off, when God takes away his life?

A hypocrite has no hope, for he believes that he or she has no soul. Our bodies are mortal, and will perish in a few years, but our souls are long lasting.

Psalms 16:9 (KJV) Therefore my heart is glad, and my glory rejoiceth: my flesh also shall rest in hope.

Hope gives rest to our body.

Psalms 22:9 (KJV) But thou art he that took me out of the womb: thou didst make me hope when I was upon my mother's breasts.

Hope can be passed on to the infant during the breast-feeding age.

Psalms 31:24 (KJV) Be of good courage, and he shall strengthen your heart, all ye that hope in the LORD.

Hope strengthens your heart. Hope is the best tonic and medicine for the heart.

Psalms 33:18-19 (KJV) 18 Behold, the eye of the LORD is upon them that fear him, upon them that hope in his mercy; 19 To deliver their soul from death, and to keep them alive in famine.

Hope is born in those who fear God, to deliver them from eternal death, and to keep them alive in famine.

Application to 'self'
Do I live a life that reflects that there is an eternal life beyond the present short mortal one?
Do I invest for the present life or for the future life?
Do I instill hope in my children and teach them absolute trust in God?

47) Samson Syndrome

Bible reference

Judges 14:1-2 (TLB) 1 One day when Samson was in Timnah he noticed a certain Philistine girl, 2 and when he got home he told his father and mother that he wanted to marry her.

Samson, a Nazarene orthodox Jew wants a Philistine wife!

Judges 14:17 (NASB77) However she wept before him seven days while their feast lasted. And it came about on the seventh day that he told her because she pressed him so hard. She then told the riddle to the sons of her people.

Betrayed by the betrothed.

Judges 16:1 (TLB) One day Samson went to the Philistine city of Gaza and spent the night with a prostitute.

Samson had a morbid fascination for Philistine women including prostitutes.

Judges 16:6 (NASB77) So Delilah said to Samson, "Please tell me where your great strength is and how you may be bound to afflict you."

Application to 'self'
　　Are my thoughts sexually pure?
　　Do I have sexual fascination for people of other religions, other nations?
　　Have I become a fornicator or adulterer in my thoughts, or actions?
　　Our own strength becomes our bitter enemy
　　When we flirt with sin "with-in you and me"
　　Self-indulgence

48) Saul Syndrome

Bible reference

1 Samuel 13:13 (NIV) "You acted foolishly," Samuel said. "You have not kept the command the Lord your God gave you; if you had, he would have established your kingdom over Israel for all time.

1 Samuel 16:14 (TLB) But the Spirit of the Lord had left Saul, and instead, the Lord had sent a tormenting spirit that filled him with depression and fear.

1 Samuel 18:8-9 (NIV) 8 Saul was very angry; this refrain galled him. "They have credited David with tens of thousands," he thought, "but me with only thousands. What more can he get but the kingdom?" 9 And from that time on Saul kept a jealous eye on David.

1 Samuel 19:9-10 (TLB) 9 But one day as Saul was sitting at home, listening to David playing the harp, suddenly the tormenting spirit from the Lord attacked him. 10 He had his spear in his hand and

hurled it at David in an attempt to kill him. But David dodged out of the way and fled into the night, leaving the spear imbedded in the timber of the wall.

1 Samuel 22:21 (KJV) And Abiathar shewed David that Saul had slain the LORD'S priests.

1 Samuel 28:7 (TLB) Saul then instructed his aides to try to find a medium so that he could ask her what to do, and they found one at Endor.

Application to 'self'
  Do I have a spirit of rebellion and disobedience?
  Am I developing a spirit of envy like the one Saul had, bringing on me a tormenting fear, and driving me to murder?
  Am I trusting in God, following the Lord Jesus, guided by the Holy Spirit or resorting to horoscopes, divination, séances, psychics and other kinds of forbidden white or black magic?

49) Scribe syndrome

Bible reference

Revelation 1:19 (TLB) Write down what you have just seen and what will soon be shown to you.

Matthew 23:29 (ASV) Woe unto you, scribes and Pharisees, hypocrites! for ye build the sepulchres of the prophets, and garnish the tombs of the righteous,

Woe unto you Scribes — Do you pass on God's message, or carry out your own massage?

Revelation 22:18-19 (KJV) 18 For I testify unto every man that heareth the words of the prophecy of this book, If any man shall add unto these things, God shall add unto him the plagues that are written in this book: 19 And if any man shall take away from the words of the book of this prophecy, God shall take away his part out of the book of life, and out of the holy city, and from the things which are written in this book.

The scribe can mediate between man and God by penning personal bias and doctrines. An honest scribe will consider the following:-

Application to 'self'
　Do I 'de cry' things, which pollute?
　Do I pre 'scribe' things, which help?
　Do I de 'scribe' things, which are true?
　Am I a God approved medium to spread the gospel?
　Do I strain at a gnat, but personally swallow a camel?
　Do I realize that I am the ass carrying God's message at this time?
　Do I desire to be an obedient, saddle 'broken' ass ready to carry the Lord?

50) Shime-I Syndrome

Bible reference

2 Samuel 16:5-8 (TLB) 5 As David and his party passed Bahurim, a man came out of the village cursing them. It was Shimei, the son of Gera, a member of Saul's family. 6 He threw stones at the king and the king's officers and all the mighty warriors who surrounded them! 7 "Get out of here, you murderer, you scoundrel!" he shouted at David. 8 "The Lord is paying you back for murdering King Saul and his family; you stole his throne and now the Lord has given it to your son Absalom! At last you will taste some of your own medicine, you murderer!"

Situation assessment
　Kick someone when you think he is down and out! This is asking for trouble – it is a self-destructive attitude. At this time, King David was running from his own son Absalom– who was trying to kill David. David could have out maneuvered and outwitted Absalom,

as David had a good following of strong seasoned warriors. He was the king. However, he loved his son and did not want to hurt his son.

Shime-I was related to Saul and was madly angry because he was no more a 'relative of the king'. He knew how King Saul was wrong and David spared Saul so often. Yet he chose to curse the King when the latter was in distress. Now, David had his guards around him. Shime-I was crazy to curse and throw stones at the King – to his face. When any one is mad, sense and caution are forgotten. Fortunately for Shimei, David spared him and spoke up in his defence.

Application to 'self'

Do I defy authority - of my boss, parents, elders, Government officers?

Do I take God for granted? Do I defy God?

Am I playing with God's mercy, His love and justice?

Am I inviting and asking for trouble?

Do I have self-destructive ways?

Do I enjoy playing with danger?

Do I enjoy playing with sin?

51) Simon the sorcerer syndrome

Bible reference

Acts 8:9 (TLB) A man named Simon had formerly been a sorcerer there for many years; he was a very influential, proud man because of the amazing things he could do—

Acts 8:17-24 (TLB) 17 Then Peter and John laid their hands upon these believers, and they received the Holy Spirit. 18 When Simon saw this—that the Holy Spirit was given when the apostles placed their hands upon people's heads—he offered money to buy this power. 19 "Let me have this power too," he exclaimed, "so that when I lay my hands on people, they will receive the Holy Spirit!" 20 But Peter replied, "Your money perish with you for thinking God's gift can be bought! 21 You can have no part in this, for your heart is not right before God. 22 Turn from this great wickedness and pray. Perhaps God will yet forgive your evil thoughts— 23 for I can see that there is jealousy and sin in your heart." 24 "Pray for me," Simon exclaimed, "that these terrible things won't happen to me."

Situation assessment
    Simon repented and therefore did not die

> He wanted to be on the stage
> And be part of the magical age

A magician is one who likes to be in the lime light. Magicians mystify people, get their applause and get to be the center of attraction. This quality tends to get ingrained into the person's behaviour.

Simon saw a greater power - the power of the Holy Spirit portrayed by the apostles, and wanted to have this power, which was greater than 'magic'. He wanted to be the center of attraction. Power of God is not for stage performers, but is given to the "age reformers"

> Simon wanted to be the 'center-stage' performer
> But God's power is given to this 'age' reformer

Application to 'self'
    Do I want to be the 'Head and not the Tail'?
    Do I want to be a leader or a servant?
    Do I feel that I am being discriminated against and need to defend myself?
    Am I upset that people wrongly abuse me and treat me as a doormat?

52) Solomon Syndrome

Bible reference

1 Kings 9:15-24 (TLB) 15 Solomon had conscripted forced labor to build the Temple, his palace, Fort Millo, the wall of Jerusalem, and the cities of Hazor, Megiddo, and Gezer.

Affluence 'cities for horses'!

1 Kings 10:26-29 (KJV) 26 And Solomon gathered together chariots and horsemen: and he had a thousand and four hundred chariots, and twelve thousand horsemen, whom he bestowed in the cities for chariots, and with the king at Jerusalem.
Sexual promiscuity

1 Kings 11:1-4 (KJV) 1 But king Solomon loved many strange women, together with the daughter of Pharaoh, women of the Moabites, Ammonites, Edomites, Zidonians, and Hittites; 2 Of the nations concerning which the LORD said unto the children of Israel, Ye shall not go in to them, neither shall they come in unto you: for surely they will turn away your heart after their gods: Solomon clave unto these in love. 3 And, he had seven hundred wives, princesses and three hundred concubines: and his wives turned away his heart. 4 For it came to pass, when Solomon was old, that his wives turned away his heart after other gods: and his heart was not perfect with the LORD his God, as was the heart of David his father.

Madness over maids
He was the wisest and the most foolish of men. He was the epitome of successful failure! For, he did not live what he preached. He chose temporal things over eternal. And at the end of his indulgent life, he wailed all was 'illusion' at his own pollution.

Made Slaves, cheated friends, short changed workers
1 Kings 11:5-8 (KJV) 5 For Solomon went after Ashtoreth the goddess of the Zidonians, and after Milcom the abomination of the Ammonites. 6 And Solomon did evil in the sight of the LORD, and went not fully after the LORD, as did David his father. 7 Then did Solomon build an high place for Chemosh, the abomination of Moab, in the hill that is before Jerusalem, and for Molech, the abomination of the children of Ammon. 8 And likewise did he for all his strange wives, which burnt incense and sacrificed unto their gods.
He began idol worship. He moved away from God in order to please his paramours.

One of the early signs or symptoms that anybody is sick is "loss of appetite"
When you lose your appetite for

1) Bible reading
2) Prayer
3) Witnessing,
you are losing your spiritual health, beginning to be sick, and getting to wander from the loving God.

Application to 'self'
    Do I have any idols in my home and my life?
    What are my recreations - TV? Movies? Story books? Socializing? Computers/ electronics?
    Am I into Idol worship or Idle worship?
    Are my appetites spiritual or carnal?
    Have I lost my appetite for spiritual things?

53) Son at Home Syndrome

Bible reference

Luke 15:25-32 (NIV) 25 "Meanwhile, the older son was in the field. When he came near the house, he heard music and dancing. 26 So he called one of the servants and asked him what was going on. 27 'Your brother has come,' he replied, 'and your father has killed the fattened calf because he has him back safe and sound.' 28 "The older brother became angry and refused to go in. So his father went out and pleaded with him. 29 But he answered his father, 'Look! All these years I've been slaving for you and never disobeyed your orders. Yet you never gave me even a young goat so I could celebrate with my friends. 30 But when this son of yours who has squandered your property with prostitutes comes home, you kill the fattened calf for him!'

31 "'My son,' the father said, 'you are always with me, and everything I have is yours. 32 But we had to celebrate and be glad, because

this brother of yours was dead and is alive again; he was lost and is found.'

Situation assessment
  Lost in the house (church)
  He was lost too, as he never found what he really needed. He never hosted his father's heart of love within him. He was 'torn' by jealously and was wild with sibling rivalry. He was angry and hints to his father that his brother had used up 'his' (prodigal's) share of his father's wealth and what was left was all his (the first son's).
  You may be a pastor or a religious person and frequent God's house but it is possible that you have not allowed God to enter into your house (your heart).

Application to 'self'
  Do I believe that I am better than another intellectually or spiritually?
  Am I 'turned-off' when I find someone badly dressed or with bad odour, enters the church and is welcomed as a VIP?
  Do I resent someone taking "my" seat at church?
  Am I resentful when the church favours someone, who I think does not deserve it?
  Do I burn with jealousy when (in my opinion) another Christian who is not worthy gets name, fame and wealth?
  Do I get upset when something is taken away from me to be given to someone I dislike or despise?
  Am I intolerant to someone, in the family, friends, acquaintance, or even a public figure?
  Am I always aware that God tolerates and loves people I don't?

54) Thyatira Church Syndrome

Bible reference

Revelation 2:18-25 (TLB) 18 "Write this letter to the leader of the church in Thyatira: "This is a message from the Son of God, whose eyes penetrate like flames of fire, whose feet are like glowing brass. 19 "I am aware of all your good deeds—your kindness to the poor, your gifts and service to them; also I know your love and faith and patience, and I can see your constant improvement in all these things. 20 "Yet I have this against you: You are permitting that woman Jezebel, who calls herself a prophetess, to teach my servants that sex sin is not a serious matter; she urges them to practice immorality and to eat meat that has been sacrificed to idols. 21 I gave her time to change her mind and attitude, but she refused. 22 Pay attention now to what I am saying: I will lay her upon a sickbed of intense affliction, along with all her immoral followers, unless they turn again to me, repenting of their sin with her; 23 and I will strike her children dead. And all the churches shall know that I am he who searches deep within men's hearts, and minds; I will give to each of you whatever you deserve. 24 "As for the rest of you in Thyatira who have not followed this false teaching ('deeper truths,' as they call them—depths of Satan, really), I will ask nothing further of you; only hold tightly to what you have until I come.

Situation assessment

Tolerating and permitting sexual perversions with self-indulgence, self-justification, ascribing such behaviour to 'genes and genetics':

Many churches have been infiltrated by ravenous wolves in sheep clothing, who occupy leading positions. They call themselves Christians, but do not believe in the Bible, or Jesus or God. They are there to plunder the money given to the church, to demonize and destroy their flock. They are loyal to their master Satan, and serve him faithfully. They are not Christians but 'Christianoid ' anti-Christians, also called as 'humaleins' in our book titled: The War of our Cultures are feeding the Vultures".

Application to 'self'

Do I believe or behave or support the theory that the Bible is wrong to say that 'homosexuality', 'adultery', 'fornication', 'drunkenness, warmongering, and lasciviousness are sins?

Do I believe that morals are a matter of cultural evolution, and need not be compatible with the Bible?

55) The Gullible Prophet of Judah
(please also see 37. Lying Prophet Syndrome)

Bible reference
1 Kings 13:8-24 (TLB)

Situation assessment
The gullible Prophet ignored God's instructions. He was 'killed' by the lion - as his defences were down. The Man of God should have known God does not go back on His Word; if the old lying prophet had injected a doubt in his mind, there was nothing to stop him from enquiring from God again, a step he sadly and fatally failed to take.

After a triumph one can trip
The prophet had just faced an angry king, stood up for God and saw the king back down. As a Christian, you should be alert for false prophets and wolves in sheep clothing and people who try to give directions. Ask God for discernment, so that you do not 'get' directed into wrong and dangerous paths.

Though the man of God had clear instructions, he allowed a liar (a so called prophet) to make him doubt God's word and disobey God.

Application to 'self'
Do I pray, seek directions for a ministry from God, and then seek human advice to carry it through?

Do I have spiritual discernment to spot false Christian advisers who expound on the 'will of God'?

When I hear from God, do I obey implicitly despite distractions and dissensions?

After any victory, our self-vanity makes us into an easy prey for the predators. The predators will change their tone, tune, melody and words once they spring the trap on their prey, like the lying Ninja prophet did.

Conclusion

If there is any need for God to operate on us, we must follow the surgical dictum which says,"when in doubt - cut it out"

1. You need to numb the part, so you can be dumb during the procedure. Humble yourself. Drop all resistance and self-will - become yielded and resigned in God's hands. He can numb the part to be 'removed' without pain to you. He takes the pain, in order to spare you the suffering. Repent and confess, as the Holy Spirit leads you.

2. Be in prayer - this is the Prophylactic/therapeutic antibiotic that brings your fever down, protects you tissues and helps in early recovery.

3. Forgive the one who caused you the grief. This allows ungluing of the offending tissue from yours, brings in an interface and capsulate the cancer so that it can be cut off - without cutting off the host (your) tissue that was harbouring the evil. Like radiation, it shrinks the inoperable mass and makes it operable and eradicable.

4. Pray for God's love to enter you, so that you can love and pray for the person who caused you the grief. This helps in rapid healing of the host tissue and confers protection from any local recurrence

5. Rejoice and give thanks - verbally and in your life. This builds up your immunity, enhances the body defence mechanism, and confers strength.

Remember:

> If this principle you will daily apply
> God, His promised cure will supply

PART 5

Self-based behavioral problems, conflicts in homes, and therapies

The role of the Bible in the science of psychology

𝒫sychology has developed into a major science since the last century, though shamans, witch doctors and charlatans who had some understanding of the human behavior and practiced their craft for centuries. In the last century, human behaviors have been accumulated, analyzed and cataloged. Unfortunately, the cure rate for sick behavior is still very poor, even according to the research and publications by well skilled academic psychologists. For psychology is a science, plagiarized from the original - the Bible – with the names of the authors excluded. The plagiarized matter made into a science has many new names and nomenclatures; however, it lacks the power for healing which the Bible has. God who was in the original version is removed from the plagiarized version, which is the reason for its impotency. The Bible is inspired into various literate and illiterate writers by God, and contains the salvaging, saving and healing power of God's Word in it operation through the Holy Spirit.

The Bible attributes human problems and sicknesses to "self" and sin. Sin is gross loss of moral (inner) hygiene. Statistics show it was only when we understood that the high human mortality rate was due to lack of physical hygiene and took steps to improve our outer hygiene that we saw change. When basic corrections were made by cleaning external filth and abstaining from drinking polluted water, the mortality rate dropped dramatically. It was not the discovery of antiseptics or any modern medical technology, which made any significant change in our mortality rate. It is the same with moral (inner) hygiene. No earthly science, however sophisticated, can cleanse our moral (inner) filth.

The Bible says that people perish for want of knowledge. The law was given in the Old Testament to let people know what is right and what is wrong. The Bible then taught that there is a penalty to pay for every sin and evil deed. God knew that humanity in every generation was incapable of refraining from sinning. Therefore, people had to be introduced to the concept of atonement for sin through blood, which is the issue of life. What God had in plan was His own sacrifice, namely that of the Lord Jesus to pay for the penalty for humanity. (Jesus was the Lamb of God to take the penalty for humanity (Isa 53:7; Jn 1:29)

For many centuries, not only the Jews, but also people of other religions around the globe resorted to ease their conscience and their guilt by offering animals or birds and their blood to atone for their guilt and sin. The priest or the witch doctor would pray to transfer the penalty from humans to the offered sacrifices. However, animal sacrifice (scapegoat) cannot cleanse our moral filth- sins, and it is only possible through the Lord Jesus who offered Himself as the sacrifice in our place. As seen earlier, Psychiatry and Psychology started as alternatives to biblical teaching, and are now incorporated into medical science. There are a few Christian psychologists and psychiatrists now, who are trying to amalgamate Psychology and the Bible. Our sciences can help in controlling our symptoms, but the ultimate healing is from God.

Even eclectic curriculums (in seminaries) have Psychology as one of the core subjects; as a result, preachers are preaching Psychology instead of the Scripture. There are medications to help assuage the symptoms, but the real cure is only through the Cross, where there is forgiveness and removal of guilt. The Cross is closely followed by the resurrection of Jesus, opening the gates of heaven and connecting us to the Holy God. The Holy Spirit offers the power to live a holy life, and to overcome sin and evil.

We use psychological terminologies, words and vocabulary in this presentation, as they are incorporated into modern day communications.

Biblical way of dealing with sin and guilt

The Bible emphasizes that every-one (whatever religion they may belong to) who wants to be cleansed and cured will have to recognize that they host moral filth, and that they need cleansing, and seek God's forgiveness. Punishing our self through self-abuse or self-immolation cannot cleanse our souls. However, because of the demands of justice, there is a penalty (blood) paid for the atonement of sin by Jesus on the cross. As we come to the Cross, we need to confess our sins as the Holy Spirit brings them to our memory (like as the patients are helped on the therapist's couch). The purpose is to get a deep cleansing, set right the internal malfunctions and make us presentable to God (not only to the society as the psycho-therapist at best hopes to do), and be able to live in cleanliness and moral health, on earth as well as in Heaven.

Following this, we should be in constant contact (follow-up) through regular prayers (our communication to God) and Bible reading (God communicating with us). The psychotherapist takes the place of God, the couch is the confessional couch (replacing the Cross) and the prize paid is cash to the therapist (instead of the free pardon by God). We all know that sin cannot go unpunished, and that someone has to take the blame and punishment. The Creator God of the Bible offers to us sinless Jesus, who volunteers to take the death penalty of sin for you and me. The science of psychology, places the blame upon the parents, society, financial status, or some other scapegoat, so that the perpetrator can feel free that he or she is blameless, and whatever he or she is, the blame lies elsewhere! The liberal legal system has accepted this kind of psychology for application of justice. Murderers and evil doers can go free, or be given royal treatment in institutions paid for by tax payers thanks to an insane "insanity clause." The psychologists can manage to cover up the dirt, making their "patients" presentable to the court and the society. On the other hand, the Bible offers the repentant sinner, power to live a morally clean life, voluntarily offering restitution for those wronged. The regenerated person learns to love his neighbors, to consider others above self, to serve God and others while on earth, drawing the strength from God on a daily basis.

The problems and dysfunctions we get into are due to lusts of the eyes, lusts of the flesh and the pride in us as the Bible says. Lust and pride are powerful emotions, which instead of assisting us to live a better life, take over control of our mind.

There are four major emotions like the four fingers in our hands, which are intimately entwined with the function of the thumb. The thumb represents the lust of our "self".

The four emotions that feed and influence the self which is the 'flesh' are :-

(1) Fear,
(2) Pride,
(3) Deception and
(4) Anger

All the other emotions, mind-set, attitude and our behavior originate from these.

From the time humans discarded alliance with God, their inner man is in darkness. The security they had under God is being replaced by Insecurity and Fear. We know that even animals and reptiles attack when terrorized. Humans become terrorists when terrorized. The 'selves' of humanity, now have become slaves to Satan's tyranny of sin, sickness and death. Self-pity has crept in with the sense of being rejected, unwilling to admit that it has only the lust of the flesh, the lust of the eyes and the pride of life to blame.

It is not by human power or might, but by the mercy and grace of God that one gets liberty and freedom from the tormenting deep-rooted emotions such as fear, guilt, grudges, pride, lust and anger.

Expressions of 'selves' in parents and children

From the beginning of this century, the roles of mothers have changed. Both parents have become wage earners to meet with the cultural change and demands. Many are becoming career minded. Depending on their priorities, either their career or their children suffer some degree of negligence, with limited personal attention and time given. Some children are gentle, others boisterous - demanding more time and care. When the parents nurture them with love, the children bond strongly with their parents. If the parents individually tend to favor one child over the other, it will initiate and aggravate sibling rivalry, which is wrong, dangerous, and harmful; it could be carried down to many generations!

If the parents go-away for a long time from the children for any reason, the separation affects the sense of security and proper maturation of the children. Some parents replace "this vital time", offering toys, TV, video games, or time filling provisions to keep the children occupied. During this time, the parents are busy all day long with work or their own toys (T.V., Internet, and other addictions). They do not want to come to grips with the truth that their children need time with them more than toys and diversions. The bonding between the parents and children are stretched beyond the limit of elasticity. The children are forced to lose their trust and dependency upon the parents. During teenage, children begin to act on their own and start their own rejection of their parent's impositions. Parents who are not sensitive to the rapid changes in their teenage children, but try to treat them as controllable possessions will cause them to become more rebellious with warped personalities. This can aggravate attacks of Insecurity in the children. The wall of security for children when breached drives fear deep within the subconscious of their young minds. The minds of the more gentle or timid ones may be affected more.

The Bible identifies fear as the 'spirit of torment'. (1 John 4:18)
The role of hope and happiness and the role of rejection
If the trials or the emotional assaults become too great, and when the anger is not erased spiritually, but is suppressed voluntarily or forcibly, hope diminishes. The internalized fear turns to anger and tries to burst intermittently like a volcanic eruption. Any person who loses hope, will feel Inadequate to deal with problems in life. That person may withdraw from people, from friends and eventually from his/her own self, feeling depressed in spirit.

The role of fear

There are two major groups of fear. One has a positive effect and the other, negative effect. Fear of God is the positive fear with awe and reverence. This fear gives us wisdom and blessings. This is a good fear to have, for it incorporates love into it.

Negative fear is termed as the 'spirit of torment' in the Bible. The Bible tells us not to fear one who can kill our bodies, but the one who can kill our souls and cast them into hell.

Every time humans encountered the supernatural, they were terrified. The angels repeatedly told people not to be overcome by fear, even when the angels brought good news. God's messengers frightened the fallen humanity.

There are three sub-groups of negative fear, which are called phobias. Phobias are morbid fear, many of them quite irrational. Phobias are often linked to the amygdala in the brain (located above the pituitary gland in the limbic lobe). The amygdala may trigger secretion of hormones, which generates fear and aggression. The adrenal medulla (situated in the adrenal glands above the right and left kidneys) secretes adrenaline setting the autonomic nervous system response, priming the subject for 'flight or fight' reaction.

(1) The first level fear will make the subject tremble, hide or flee. The fear phobias commonly experienced are

- for thunder (Astrophobia, Brontophobia)
- for tornado (Lilapsophobia)
- stage-fright (Topophobia)

- open space (Agoraphobia)
- crowds of people (Anthropophobia)

These are panic-fears resulting in flight

(2) The second level fears are those that give us an aversion for and make us avoid:

- fear and dislike of spiders (Arachnophobia)
- fear and dislike for insects (Entemophobia)
- fear and aversion for cats (Ailurophobia)
- fear and aversion for reptile (Herpetophobia)

This kind of fear results in aversion and avoidance (shunning) = "repel-shun".

(3) Examples of the third level fears are:

- fear, dislike and hatred of Jews (Judeo-phobia)
- fear, dislike and hatred for foreigners (Xenophobia)

The third level of fears produces an intense dislike, hatred, anger and manic-rage leading to persecutions and war (fight)

Fear produces a sense of inadequacy for interviews, resulting in loss of trust of people and may be even jobs. Those thus affected avoid working in an organization. There are phobias arising out of the combination of fear, and inadequacy, resulting in insecurity. Those who are not strong minded, or timid suffer an inferiority complex. For others, fear may trigger a retaliation reaction with anger and violent aggression. In some, a pendulum effect starts with panic attacks, to which the normal inbuilt autonomous physiological response is either a flight a fright reaction, or possibly a fight reaction.

Fear really creates anger due to the adrenal rush. This reaction is almost instantaneous and spontaneous. When fear is not overcome, the person can go into torments of depression. Repetition of fright incidences can produce panic attacks followed by manic responses.

The autonomous response is due to the sympathetic nervous system of the body, which acts upon the endocrine glands, especially the medulla of the adrenal glands. It is difficult to control autonomic spontaneous reaction by our voluntary effort, and we certainly need Divine help to do so. Uncontrolled adrenalin rushes will damage many internal organs, and produce adverse changes in the blood and blood vessels with elevation of blood pressure and changes in the blood chemistry. Sudden rise in blood pressure can result in a dangerous stress, causing heart attack or rupture of blood vessel in brain, causing a stroke. To combat the effects of adrenaline, Cortisol from adrenal cortex is released into the blood. When there is excess of Cortisol, it produces depression by its action on the brain. Anxiety and stress (due to sympathetic system reaction) are added to the deadly formula of stress with tension. This, as seen earlier, is the reason heart attacks and strokes are becoming more common. Parental contributions to their progeny are not only due to transfer of bad genes, but also bad legacy of insecurity, inadequacy and other personality conflicts. In severe cases of people thus affected by fear, their faith is shaken not only in human beings, but also even in God. The physiological homeostatic balancing reaction brings in cortisol to balance the effect of adrenaline. When Cortisol effects are prolonged, depression sets in, and the brain needs to increase the level of Serotonin in the brain to combat depression. When faith becomes weak, hope and trust suffer also. Discipline, obedience, steadfastness and commitments will appear to be of no value to one sinking into rejection. It surely brings pain and suffering into every one in the family who cares and loves them. This is what happens inside children. As children grow into adulthood, they could develop the following dysfunctions in their own life.

(1) The person may be afraid (fearful) to make commitments, fearing possible rejection from people. If they subconsciously perceive (rightly or wrongly) that their parents failed to protect them or their siblings from someone who was abusing them, physically or emotionally, they get discouraged, disillusioned and sink into deep depression and despair, resulting from loss of trust leading to Insecurity.

Self-Based Behavioral Problems, And Conflicts.....

(2) In some, Fear may lead to anger. When not expressed, vented out, or demonstrated, it leads to discouragement and depression.

The above two powerful, deep seated negative emotions tend to produce a sense of Inferiority and Self-pity, which would be carried to adulthood when they have families of their own. Anxiety and stress follow them, hindering happy, productive and useful lives. In extreme situations, even getting a job may bring panic (for fear of being hurt again by the co-workers and rejected); even though people thus affected are more than capable, they suffer a feeling of Inadequacy.

Thus, fear and panic can cause three crippling emotions, namely, insecurity, inadequacy and inferiority complex. All these will result in production of anger due to our built in homeostatic mechanism. This will result in a change of our conduct, which if not corrected in time will cause a change in character for the worse. This will further deteriorate into bad behavior. Behavior will determine the attitude, and the attitude will determine our identification. Our identification becomes incorporated into our personality and even our eventual destination.

The role of anger

Most wars are due to fear. As we mentioned earlier, the third level of negative fear results in persecutions and war. This combination robs the sanity of people, making them angry, starting quarrels and wars. Evil individuals who worm their way into politics or religion will use this weakness to recruit suicide bombers. This terror-training maneuver has further terrorized all the nations in the world. The travel pleasures of the past years are replaced by costly, cautious, delayed, expensive hassles filled evil.

Anger causes stress, hurting the person who is angry, more than the recipient of the anger.

> Stress when added to existing stress,
> Will surely make you experience Distress.

Anger in a man is like having a few cancer cells in the body which endanger the entire billions of cells in the body. These negative emotions form a vicious cycle of Fear and Anger due to the endocrinal take-over; producing panic attacks followed by manic response. The autonomic nervous system automatically tries to correct the panic reaction. This often ends up as an over correction, leading to manic reactions with violence in thoughts, speech and actions

This phenomenon through the built in Sympathetic Autonomous nervous system reaction is addressed as Bipolar disorder in psychiatry books.

Role models

Some of the children when grown into adulthood may want to run away and abandon their own family and children like their parent did. They may find many excuses and reasons for doing so, not willing to face their subconscious inner man and 'self'. It does not mean that they lack love. They love their 'self' more than they love others, and indulge themselves self-centeredly.

This may be because children re-enact their parents. Parents whether they know it, like it, or not, may see their children mimicking themselves in their adult lives! They do become their children's role models! Parenthood is indeed an awesome responsibility, and alas only a few parents make the grade - only those who understand that their children are only a loan from God, and that the parents are like the temporary baby sitters!

Sibling rivalry

Sibling rivalry is the generational curse upon humanity. If unchecked and not brought to the Cross on a daily basis, it will result as it did between Cain and Abel, Joseph and his brothers, or Jacob and Esau to mention a few. There is competition, jealousy, envy and greed brewed together in sibling rivalry. There is also a love-hate relationship. When there is an external threat, the siblings will come together in unity against the opponents. However, each one of the siblings wants to be the chief or the leader, and receive the best benefits, and obeisance from the rest. Like the alpha animal in canines, the 'boss' child is defensive of the rest of the siblings when a common foe approaches.

Miscommunication of the pain of guilt or hurts

Any onlooker may think that adults who do not show signs of maturity are mentally sick, or mentally handicapped, or very selfish or self-centered. However, they may not realize that the persons may be hurting, and miscommunicate the pain. God said that we should cast our cares and burdens upon Him, for He can read our emotional pain whether we communicate it or not.

> When one does not know how to tell,
> Will end up at other people to yell

Daily visit to the Cross is like our visit to the mirror where we will be 'shown' our errors. If we admit to our problem without covering up or justifying ourselves, and willing to be treated by God, we will be healed completely of all blemishes, dysfunctions, and restored to normal function, and become a blessing to all.

To illustrate mis-communication, I will narrate two true incidences:

1) A two-year-old child started crying and screaming in the night, and the parents thought that it was due to a temper tantrum. It was many hours later in the light of the day that they realized that the child was having an acute ear infection. There was severe swelling which needed medical care. Even an adult on pain medication could not have tolerated that pain.

2) There was a 10 year old, slightly mentally retarded boy in India, who after putting on his shoes before going to school started screaming and crying. He could not communicate properly the reason for crying, and the parents thought that he did not want to go to school and was being difficult. After some time, he became unconscious, and as he was admitted into the hospital; and as his shoes were removed, the cause of his problem became obvious. There was a scorpion in the shoe, and it had stung the boy multiple times. The poor boy never came out of the coma, and died.

As the child could not talk, the only way he could tell the parents he was in pain was to cry. Even the concerned parent could not understand it. To reiterate:

> Those who are unable to "tell"
> May only cry or annoyingly "yell"

Practical-clinical application

Self-evaluation by parents can reveal how they had failed the children who depended on them. Children specially emulate the father figure subconsciously. Whenever parents find fault with the way their children behave and live, they must remember and realize the major role they themselves had played in the past, and remember, 'what goes around, comes around'.

The parental prayer should be "God have mercy, let not our children emulate us. Help them to emulate only Thee our Heavenly Father. To do this, they need Thy mercy and grace".

However, this information is not to be used for finding someone else to blame. Each person - be it the father, or the mother, or the child or the sibling - each individual is personally accountable to God, who sees through all shams and sophistication, into our inner most motives and sins.

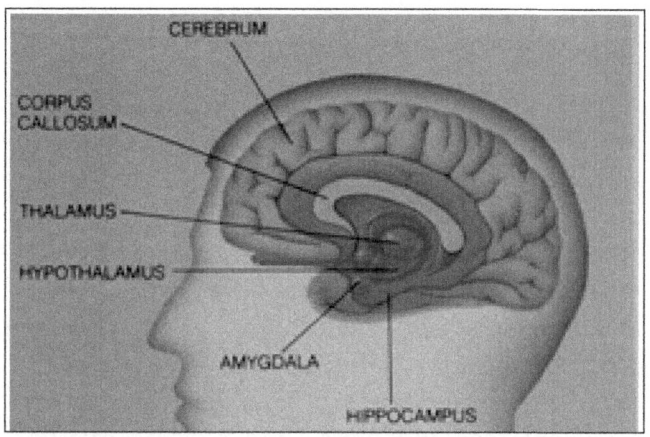

Frontal lobe and Amygdala are affected by phobic fears

For those who want more information and medical data:

The information given below is only to those who want more scientific correlation. Most psychological patients are supposed to be afflicted due to mental disease. The mind is not an anatomical structure, as our brain is. Our thoughts and imaginations however arise from the mind. The brain is a composite of fatty neurons with trillions of nerve fibers and synaptic junctions. There are different areas of brain, which seem to produce an excess of neuro humeral, or use up selective neuro humeral. We realize that bad negative emotions affect the brain. Neuro-scientists have recorded neuro-humeral changes, seen during the negative emotions and other situations and have analyzed the cause (the negative emotions) and effect (the abnormal behavior). Psychiatrists treat the patient with chemicals to balance the neuro-humeral fluctuations. They have no power to control peoples' emotions or their behavior. All a Psychiatrist can do is to use drugs that will suppress, or stimulate the patients by altering the neurochemical balance. If there is low brain Serotonin turnover rate, it is indicated by low concentration of 5-Hydroxy indole acetic acid (5-HIAA) in the Cerebro-spinal-fluid (CSF). The effect of this is upon the Supra-chiasmatic nucleus in the Hypo Thalamus. This area is involved in the maintenance of Circadian rhythm and blood sugar level. Therefore, our negative emotions cause sleep disorders. Low sugar damages the Amygdala as well as the frontal brain cortex. Emotions of fears and frustrations are perceived by the Amygdala and hippocampus. The Amygdala, the adjacent brain-stem, hypothalamus, and cerebellum also process fear and anxiety. They act on the pituitary gland located beneath them, influencing the autonomic nervous system, and involve the cortical grey matter of the brain where we store our memories. Thus, whenever 'that specific situation' is met with again, the body reacts as if the event was happening immediately. Low levels of GABA, a neurotransmitter that reduces activity in the central nervous system, contribute to anxiety. Low 5-HIAA may be hereditary.

Those suffering from generalized anxiety often experience non-specific persistent fear and worry and become overly concerned with everyday matters. In panic disorder, a person suffers from brief attacks of intense terror and apprehension, often marked by trembling, shaking, confusion, dizziness, nausea, or difficulty in breathing. Panic attacks may arise abruptly and peak in less than ten minutes. They can last for several hours and can be triggered by stress, fear, or even exercise; the specific cause is not always apparent. The person fears and avoids whatever situation might induce a panic attack. He or she rarely leaves home to prevent a panic attack causing inescapable, extreme terror (agoraphobia).

Obsessive–compulsive disorder (OCD) is a type of anxiety disorder primarily characterized by repetitive obsessions and compulsions with uncontrollable urges to perform specific acts or rituals. Post-traumatic stress disorder is an anxiety disorder, which results from a traumatic experience. Post-traumatic stress can result from an extreme incidence, such as combat, rape, child abuse, or even a serious accident. It can also result from long term (chronic) exposure to a severe stress. Common symptoms are avoidant behaviors, anxiety, anger and depression.

Separation anxiety disorder is the feeling of excessive and inappropriate levels of anxiety over being separated from a person or place. Separation anxiety is a normal part of development in babies or children, and it is only when this feeling is excessive or inappropriate that it can be considered a disorder. Separation anxiety disorder affects roughly 7% of adults. Death of one or both parents in childhood can affect the person even during adulthood.

Children as well as adults worry and fear when facing different situations, especially those involving a new experience, but such anxiety should only be temporary and must not interfere with the subject's normal functioning or maturing. When subjects suffer from a severe anxiety disorder (phobia), their thinking, decision making ability, perceptions of the environment, learning and concentration get affected. They not only experience fear, nervousness, and shyness but also start avoiding places and activities. Anxiety raises blood pressure and heart rate. Nausea, vomiting, stomach pain, ulcers, diarrhea, tingling, weakness, and shortness of breath may occur due to anxiety. Other symptoms are frequent 'self-involvement with hyperactivity, inattentiveness, attention deficit disorders, irritability, sleep problems, eating disorders, depression, substance abuse, and, in extreme cases, suicidal thoughts. Children with a parent with anxiety disorders are likely to develop an anxiety disorder too. Stress can trigger anxiety disorders.

Allopathic palliative drugs for negative emotions

Psychologists adopt gradual desensitization treatment and cognitive behavioral therapy. They use Antidepressant medications such, MAOIs, and Benzodiazepines and find them to be helpful in cases of phobias. Then there are Tricyclic antidepressants with selective Serotonin reuptake inhibitors (SSRIs) ; but these drugs have significant to dangerous side reactions. Prevention method in treating stress and anxiety is to have regular aerobic exercise, improving sleep, hygiene, avoiding coffee, alcohols and other stimulants.

Selective serotonin reuptake inhibitors are commonly used to treat anxiety with depression. Caffeine especially coffee, alcohol and benzodiazepine can cause anxiety and panic attacks or worsen them. Stimulants are likely to cause repetitive panic attacks. There is evidence that chronic exposure to organic solvents like paints and varnishes triggers fear and anxiety disorders.

Herbal palliative help for emotional problems

Herbal remedies like butterbur, valerian root, passionflower, lemon balm leaf, kava, St. John's wort and Inositol are sometimes used. They are said to have modest benefit in patients with panic disorder or obsessive-compulsive disorder.

The spiritual method – curative

The Bible promises that perfect love will cast out all fear. Perfect love was demonstrated only at the Cross, where Jesus the Lord of Creation came to offer the miserable sin and sickness-laden, death-bound humankind forgiveness, healing and eternal life. It was upon the Cross that Jesus forgave those who were persecuting and putting Him to death, out of love. In 1 Corinthians 13th Chapter we see that gentleness, kindness, patience, endurance, hope, trust, and faith, are built into love. Self-evaluation as a family, with individual communication between Parents and Children, with Jesus as the Mediator (Prince of Peace) will bring healing, peace and joy into individuals and families whenever they hurt. Each one needs to come to the foot of the Cross, and repent and be willing to forgive those who had hurt or offended them, and be humble enough to wash one another's feet, just like Jesus the Lord did. The love of God will cast out fear and all associated dysfunctions. If one believes, trusts the Lord, and has faith, he / she will find a cure that modern science does not have for bad emotions.

Hope and faith are the two blessings, which have a huge effect on us, and are able to bring peace within us, whether the winds are ferocious or the waves tossing high. The Prince of peace resides within His followers and brings 'homeostasis'; He calms the emotional storms. His presence in our lives will remove pride and bring willingness to forgive others as He did.

When the inner man is having peace, the outer man (Amygdala and the autonomic system) should also enjoy peace.

Love for God will transform into love of God in our inner man, and will enable us to love our neighbors regardless of who they are or what they are.

To summarize:-

1) There are four deep negative emotions, which affect, influence or control the 'self'. The self may be considered as the thumb. The four fingers of emotion are Fear, Pride, Deception and Retaliation (anger, bitterness, and unwillingness to forgive others).
2) All of us humans tend to reject one another, including our own selves. This leads to self-pity. Self-pity combines Inferiority complex, which may put on an outer garment of superiority. Our Insecurity may show an outward bluster; and our feeling of Inadequacy can open doors for self-indulgence, and excuses for our various 'selves'.
3) It will be great blessing if each one of us carries the Mirror of Cross with us on a constant basis, like many ladies carry a compact mirror and use it many times a day.

Prayer

Almighty God, please open my inner (real) eyes to realize and recognize if I have any of these 'biblical syndromes' with many self-cantered "selves". Even if there be a least symptom of 'self', help me to repent and come to Thee with deep contrition and humility for forgiveness and removal of 'self'. Help me not to ignore or cover up my symptoms and sins only to suffer the consequences. Heal me and my family members from all dysfunctions and syndromes of 'self'. Please let my 'self and flesh' be nailed to the backside of thy Cross, so that people will see only Thee as they themselves come to the Cross with their own needs.

Remove from me negative passions like overwhelming fear, anger, lust, pride, covetousness and bitterness.

Let me not host 'self-indulgences', and help me avoid putting on masquerading make-ups. The make-up of 'selves' I put on as cover ups, are causing severe allergic reactions, making it hard for me even to breathe properly. They also make it harder to get 'inspiration' from Thee my God. Help me to consecrate myself in full surrender. Remove from me my tendency to wriggle out of your altar, blaming that the altar is too hard or cold.

I ask this in the name of Jesus whom you sent for me, and who gave His whole "self" for me. Amen.

References

1) The Bible references using Word Search 10 NavPress
   I Exalt Electronic Publishing

2) Self-Confrontation Developed by John C. Borger
   Biblical counseling Training Program
   Capstone Publishers. LTD Hong Kong. December 1996
3) Who is who in the Bible?

4) How to Resolve 7 Deadly Stresses
   A health Manual for All Nations
   Published by the Institute in Basic Life Principles .INC
   Oak Brook IL 60522

5) Topical guide to the Bible (NIV)
   Edited by Walter A. Elwell
   Published by Baker Books
   P.O. Box 6287, Grand Rapids, MI 49516-6287

6) Psycho Heresy. The Psychological Seduction of Christianity
   Martin and Deidre Bobgan
   East Gate Publishers.
   Santa Barbara, CA 93110

7) Psychology
   Spencer A. Rathus

Harcourt Brace College Publishers
Fort Worth TX 76102

8) Psycholgy The Fundamentals of Human Adjustment
Norman L. Munn University of Adelaide
Houghton Mifflin Company Boston

9) Abnormal Psychology A New Look
Mashall P. Duke & Stephen Nowicki, Jr
CBS College Publishing

10) Wikipedia

Grateful Acknowledgement

*R*ev. Douglas Friederichsen for use of the illustrations from the five great-illustrated study books (1. God's Relief for Burdens. 2. God's Will Made Clear. 3. God's Way Made Easy. 4. God's Truth Made Simple. 5. God's Word Made Plain, by Mrs. Paula Kay Friederichsen, mother of Rev. Douglas); and the publishers, Moody press

Trivia which may interest some:-
The Bible defines' fear as a tormenting spirit'. Psychiatry coined new words to fit different types of fears. They used Latin names ending with the word "phobia". The newly coined words became the currency in all English speaking countries. The explosion of internet has resulted in the minting of some more new words to describe fear, attaching the letters phobia to them. Many of these fears can become obsessive. In such cases, instead of the subjects being possessed with fear, fear possesses them. A phobia is a type of anxiety disorder due to a persistent morbid fear of an object or situation. The cause of such fear may be real or imaginary. However the reaction is out of normal, eliciting an abnormal behavioral response. The behavior is irrational, with severe emotional distress causing impairment of their activity, affecting their daily life as well as their social interaction.

Phobia is either a specific phobia or a social phobia. There is a huge list of phobias, with their numbers ever increasing. Please refer to Wikipedia or Google search for details. We will list some of them here:

A list of Phobias (Fear) from Wikipedia

FEAR OF (Phobias):
13 (number)- Triskadekaphobia.
666 (number)- Hexakosioihexekontahexaphobia
8 (number)- Octophobia
The fear of long words is known as hippopotomonstrosesquippedaliophobia

A -

Abuse: sexual- Contreltophobia.
Accidents- Dystychiphobia.
Air- Anemophobia.
Air swallowing- Aerophobia.
Airborne noxious substances- Aerophobia.
Airsickness- Aeronausiphobia.
Alcohol- Methyphobia or Potophobia.
Alone, being- Autophobia or Monophobia.
Alone, being or solitude- Isolophobia.
Amnesia- Amnesiphobia.
Anger- Angrophobia or Cholerophobia.
Angina- Anginophobia.
Animals- Zoophobia.
Animals, skins of or fur- Doraphobia.
Animals, wild- Agrizoophobia.

Ants- Myrmecophobia.
Anything new- Neophobia.
Asymmetrical things- Asymmetriphobia
Atomic Explosions- Atomosophobia.
Automobile, being in a moving- Ochophobia.
Automobiles- Motorphobia.

B -

Bacteria- Bacteriophobia.
Bald people- Peladophobia.
Bald, becoming- Phalacrophobia.
Bathing- Ablutophobia.
Bats- Chiroptophobia.
Beards- Pogonophobia.
Beaten by a rod or instrument of punishment, or of being severely criticized- Rhabdophobia.
Beautiful women- Caligynephobia.
Beds or going to bed- Clinophobia.

Bees- Apiphobia or Melissophobia.
Belly buttons- Omphalophobia.
Bicycles- Cyclophobia.
Birds- Ornithophobia.
Black- Melanophobia.
Blindness in a visual field- Scotomaphobia.
Blood- Hemophobia, Hemaphobia or Hematophobia.
Blushing or the color red- Erythrophobia, Erytophobia or Ereuthophobia.
Body odors- Osmophobia or Osphresiophobia.
Body, things to the left side of the body- Levophobia.
Body, things to the right side of the body- Dextrophobia.
Bogeyman or bogies- Bogyphobia.
Bolsheviks- Bolshephobia.
Books- Bibliophobia.
Bound or tied up- Merinthophobia.
Bowel movements: painful- Defecaloesiophobia.

Brain disease- Meningitophobia.
Bridges or of crossing them- Gephyrophobia.
Buildings: being close to high buildings- Batophobia.
Bullets- Ballistophobia.
Bulls- Taurophobia.
Bums or beggars- Hobophobia.
Burglars, or being harmed by wicked persons- Scelerophobia.
Buried alive, being or cemeteries- Taphephobia or Taphophobia.

C -

Cancer- Cancerophobia, Carcinophobia.
Car or vehicle, riding in- Amaxophobia.
Cats- Aclurophobia, Ailurophobia, Elurophobia, Felinophobia, Galeophobia, or Gatophobia.
Celestial spaces- Astrophobia.
Cemeteries- Coimetrophobia.
Cemeteries or being buried alive- Taphephobia or Taphophobia.
Ceremonies, religious- Teleophobia.
Changes, making; moving- Tropophobia or Metathesiophobia.
Chickens- Alektorophobia.
Child, bearing a deformed; deformed people- Teratophobia.
Childbirth- Maleusiophobia, Tocophobia, Parturiphobia, or Lockiophobia.
Children- Pedophobia.
Chinese or Chinese culture- Sinophobia.
Chins- Geniophobia.
Choking or being smothered- Pnigophobia or Pnigerophobia.
Choking- Anginophobia.
Cholera- Cholerophobia.
Chopsticks- Consecotaleophobia.
Church- Ecclesiophobia.
Clocks- Chronomentrophobia.
Clocks or time- Chronophobia.
Clothing- Vestiphobia.
Clouds- Nephophobia.
Clowns- Coulrophobia.

Coitus- Coitophobia.
Cold or cold things- Frigophobia.
Cold: extreme, ice or frost- Cryophobia.
Cold- Cheimaphobia, Cheimatophobia, Psychrophobia or Psychropophobia.
Color purple- Porphyrophobia.
Color red or blushing- Erythrophobia, Erytophobia or Ereuthophobia.
Color yellow- Xanthophobia.
Color white- Leukophobia.
Colors- Chromophobia or Chromatophobia.
Comets- Cometophobia.
Computers or working on computers- Cyberphobia.
Confined spaces- Claustrophobia.
Constipation- Coprastasophobia.
Contamination, dirt or infection- Molysmophobia or Molysomophobia.
Contamination with dirt or germs- Misophobia or Mysophobia.
Cooking- Mageirocophobia.
Corpses- Necrophobia.
Cosmic Phenomenon- Kosmikophobia.
Creepy, crawly things- Herpetophobia.
Criticized severely, or beaten by rod or instrument of punishment- Rhabdophobia.
Criticism- Enissophobia.
Crosses or the crucifix- Staurophobia.
Crossing streets- Agyrophobia or Dromophobia.
Crowded public places like markets- Agoraphobia.
Crowds or mobs- Enochlophobia, Demophobia or Ochlophobia.
Crucifix, the or crosses- Staurophobia.
Crystals or glass- Crystallophobia.

D -

Dampness, moisture or liquids- Hygrophobia.
Dancing- Chorophobia.
Dark or night- Nyctophobia.

A List Of Phobias (Fear) From Wikipedia

Dark place, being in- Lygophobia.
Darkness- Achluophobia or Myctophobia, or Scotophobia.
Dawn or daylight- Eosophobia.
Daylight or sunshine- Phengophobia.
Death or dying- Thanatophobia.
Death or dead things- Necrophobia.
Decaying matter- Seplophobia.
Decisions: making decisions- Decidophobia.
Defeat- Kakorrhaphiophobia.
Deformed people or bearing a deformed child- Teratophobia.
Deformity or unattractive body image- Dysmorphophobia.
Demons- Demonophobia or Daemonophobia.
Dental surgery- Odontophobia.
Dentists- Dentophobia.
Dependence on others- Soteriophobia.
Depth- Bathophobia.
Diabetes- Diabetophobia.
Dining or dinner conversations- Deipnophobia.
Dirt, contamination or infection- Molysmophobia or Molysomophobia.
Dirt or germs, being contaminated with- Misophobia or mysophobia.
Dirt or filth- Rhypophobia or Rupophobia.
Dirty, being dirty or personal filth- Automysophobia.
Disease- Nosophobia, Nosemaphobia or Pathophobia.
Disease and suffering- Panthophobia.
Disease, a definite- Monopathophobia.
Disease, brain- Meningitophobia.
Disease: kidney- Albuminurophobia.
Disease, rectal- Rectophobia.
Disorder or untidiness- Ataxophobia.
Dizziness or vertigo when looking down- Illyngophobia.
Dizziness or whirlpools- Dinophobia.
Doctor, going to the- Iatrophobia.
Doctrine, challenges to or radical deviation from official- Heresyphobia or Hereiophobia.
Dogs or rabies- Cynophobia.

Dolls- Pediophobia.
Double vision- Diplophobia.
Drafts- Aerophobia or Anemophobia.
Dreams, wet- Oneirogmophobia.
Dreams- Oneirophobia.
Drinking- Dipsophobia.
Drugs, new- Neopharmaphobia.
Drugs or taking medicine- Pharmacophobia.
Dryness- Xerophobia.
Dust- Amathophobia or Koniophobia.
Dust- Amathophobia.
Duty or responsibility, neglecting- Paralipophobia.
Dying or death- Thanatophobia.

E -

Eating or swallowing- Phagophobia.
Eating or food- Sitophobia or Sitiophobia.
Eating or swallowing or of being eaten- Phagophobia.
Eight, the number- Octophobia.
Electricity- Electrophobia.
Englishness- Anglophobia.
Erect penis- Medorthophobia.
Erection, losing an- Medomalacuphobia.
Everything- Panophobia, Panphobia, Pamphobia, or Pantophobia.
Eyes- Ommetaphobia or Ommatophobia.
Eyes, opening one's- Optophobia..

F -

Fabrics, certain- Textophobia.
Failure- Atychiphobia or Kakorrhaphiophobia.
Fainting- Asthenophobia.
Fatigue- Kopophobia.
Fearful situations: being preferred by a phobic- Counterphobia.
Feathers or being tickled by feathers- Pteronophobia.
Fecal matter, feces- Coprophobia or Scatophobia.

Female genitals- Kolpophobia.
Female genitalia- Eurotophobia.
Fever- Febriphobia, Fibriphobia, Fidriophobia or Pyrexiophobia.
Filth or dirt- Rhypophobia.
Fire- Arsonphobia or Pyrophobia.
Firearms- Hoplophobia.
Fish- Ichthyophobia.
Flashes- Selaphobia.
Flogging or punishment- Mastigophobia.
Floods- Antlophobia.
Flowers- Anthrophobia or Anthophobia.
Flutes- Aulophobia.
Flying- Aviophobia or Aviatophobia or Pteromerhanophobia.
Fog- Homichlophobia or Nebulaphobia.
Food or eating- Sitophobia or Sitiophobia.
Food- Cibophobia.
Foreigners or strangers- Xenophobia.
Foreign languages- Xenoglossophobia.
Forests or wooden objects- Xylophobia.
Forests- Hylophobia.
Forests, dark wooded area, of at night- Nyctohylophobia
Forgetting or being forgotten- Athazagoraphobia.
France or French culture- Francophobia, Gallophobia or Galiphobia.
Freedom- Eleutherophobia.
Friday the 13th- Paraskavedekatriaphobia.
Frogs- Batrachophobia.
Frost, ice or extreme cold- Cryophobia.
Frost or ice- Pagophobia.
Functioning or work: surgeon's fear of operating- Ergasiophobia.
Fur or skins of animals- Doraphobia.

G -

Gaiety- Cherophobia.
Garlic- Alliumphobia.
Genitals, particularly female- Kolpophobia.

Genitalia, female- Eurotophobia.
Germans or German culture- Germanophobia or Teutophobia.
Germs or dirt, being contaminated with- Misophobia or mysophobia.
Germs- Verminophobia.
Ghosts or specters- Spectrophobia.
Ghosts- Phasmophobia.
Girls, young or virgins- Parthenophobia.
Glass or crystals- Crystallophobia.
Glass- Hyelophobia, Hyalophobia or Nelophobia.
Gloomy place, being in- Lygophobia.
God or gods- Zeusophobia.
Gods or religion- Theophobia.
Gold- Aurophobia.
Good news, hearing good news- Euphobia.
Gravity- Barophobia.
Greek or Greek culture- Hellophobia.
Greek terms- Hellenologophobia.

H -

Hair- Chaetophobia, Trichopathophobia, Trichophobia, or Hypertrichophobia.
Halloween- Samhainophobia.
Hands- Chirophobia.
Handwriting- Graphophobia.
Harmed by wicked persons; bad men or burglars- Scelerophobia.
Heart- Cardiophobia.
Heat- Thermophobia.
Heaven- Ouranophobia or Uranophobia.
Heights- Acrophobia, Altophobia, Batophobia, Hypsiphobia or Hyposophobia.
Hell- Hadephobia, Stygiophobia or Stigiophobia.
Heredity- Patroiophobia.
Hoarding- Disposophobia.
Holy things- Hagiophobia.
Home- Ecophobia.

Home surroundings or a house- Oikophobia.
Home, returning- Nostophobia.
Home surroundings- Eicophobia.
Homosexuality or of becoming homosexual- Homophobia.
Horses- Equinophobia or Hippophobia.
Hospitals- Nosocomephobia.
House or home surroundings- Oikophobia.
Houses or being in a house- Domatophobia.
Hurricanes and tornadoes- Lilapsophobia.
Hypnotized, being or of sleep- Hypnophobia.

I -

Ice or frost- Pagophobia.
Ice, frost or extreme cold- Cryophobia.
Ideas- Ideophobia.
Ignored, being- Athazagoraphobia.
Imperfection- Atelophobia.
Inability to stand- Basiphobia or Basophobia.
Infection, contamination or dirt- Molysmophobia or Molysomophobia.
Infinity- Apeirophobia.
Injections- Trypanophobia.
Injury- Traumatophobia.
Insanity, dealing with- Lyssophobia.
Insanity- Dementophobia or Maniaphobia.
Insects- Acarophobia or Entomophobia or Insectophobia.
Insects that eat wood- Isopterophobia.
Insects that cause itching- Acarophobia.
Itching- Acarophobia.

J -

Japanese or Japanese culture- Japanophobia.
Jealousy- Zelophobia.
Jews- Judeophobia.
Joint immobility- Ankylophobia.

Jumping from high and low places- Catapedaphobia.
Justice- Dikephobia.

K -

Kidney disease- Albuminurophobia.
Kissing- Philemaphobia or Philematophobia.
Knees- Genuphobia.
Knowledge- Gnosiophobia or Epistemophobia.
L-
Lakes- Limnophobia.
Large things- Megalophobia.
Laughter- Geliophobia.
Lawsuits- Liticaphobia.
Learning- Sophophobia.
Left-handed; objects at the left side of the body- Sinistrophobia.
Leprosy- Leprophobia or Lepraphobia.
Lice- Pediculophobia or Phthiriophobia.
Light- Photophobia.
Light flashes- Selaphobia.
Lightning and thunder- Brontophobia or Karaunophobia.
Lights, glaring- Photoaugliaphobia.
Liquids, dampness or moisture- Hygrophobia.
Locked in an enclosed place- Cleithrophobia, Cleisiophobia, or Clithrophobia.
Lockjaw or tetanus- Tetanophobia.
Loneliness or of being oneself- Eremophobia or Eremiphobia.
Looking up- Anablephobia or Anablepophobia.
Loud noises- Ligyrophobia.
Love, sexual love- Erotophobia.
Love play- Malaxophobia or Sarmassophobia.
Love, falling or being in- Philophobia.

M -

Machines- Mechanophobia.
Mad, becoming- Lyssophobia.

A List Of Phobias (Fear) From Wikipedia

Many things- Polyphobia.
Marriage- Gamophobia.
Materialism- Hylephobia.
Matter, decaying- Seplophobia.
Meat- Carnophobia.
Medicine, taking; or drugs- Pharmacophobia.
Medicines, mercurial- Hydrargyophobia.
Medicine, prescribing by a doctor- Opiophobia.
Memories- Mnemophobia.
Men, bad or burglars or being harmed by wicked persons- Scelerophobia.
Men- Androphobia or Arrhenphobia or Hominophobia.
Menstruation- Menophobia.
Mercurial medicines- Hydrargyophobia.
Metal- Metallophobia.
Meteors- Meteorophobia.
Mice- Musophobia, Murophobia or Suriphobia.
Microbes- Bacillophobia or Microbiophobia.
Mind- Psychophobia.
Mirrors or seeing oneself in a mirror- Eisoptrophobia.
Mirrors- Catoptrophobia.
Missiles- Ballistophobia.
Mobs or crowds- Demophobia, Enochlophobia or Ochlophobia.
Moisture, dampness or liquids- Hygrophobia.
Money- Chrometophobia or Chrematophobia.
Moon- Selenophobia.
Mother-in-law- Pentheraphobia.
Moths- Mottephobia.
Motion or movement- Kinetophobia or Kinesophobia.
Moving or making changes- Tropophobia.
Moving automobile or vehicle, being in- Ochophobia.
Muscular incoordination (Ataxia)- Ataxiophobia.
Mushrooms- Mycophobia.
Music- Melophobia.
Myths or stories or false statements- Mythophobia.

N -

Names or hearing a certain name- Onomatophobia.
Names- Nomatophobia.
Narrow things or places- Stenophobia.
Narrowness- Anginophobia.
Needles- Aichmophobia or Belonephobia.
New, anything or novel- Kainophobia, Kainolophobia, Cenophobia, Centophobia, or Neophobia.
Newness- Cainophobia, Cenophobia, Centophobia, or Cainotophobia.
News: hearing good news- Euphobia.
Night or dark- Nyctophobia.
Night- Noctiphobia.
Noise- Acousticophobia.
Noises, loud- Ligyrophobia.
Noises or voices, speaking aloud, or telephones- Phonophobia.
Northern lights- Auroraphobia.
Nosebleeds- Epistaxiophobia.
Novelty or anything new- Kainophobia or Kainolophobia.
Novelty- Cainophobia or Cainotophobia.
Nuclear weapons- Nucleomituphobia.
Nudity- Gymnophobia or Nudophobia.
Number 8- Octophobia.
Number 13- Triskadekaphobia.
Numbers- Arithmophobia or Numerophobia.

O -

Objects, small- Tapinophobia.
Ocean or sea- Thalassophobia.
Odor, personal- Bromidrosiphobia, Bromidrophobia, Osmophobia or Osphresiophobia.
Odor, that one has a vile odor- Autodysomophobia.
Odors or smells- Olfactophobia.
Official doctrine, challenges to or radical deviation from- Heresyphobia or Hereiophobia.

A List Of Phobias (Fear) From Wikipedia

Old people- Gerontophobia.
Old, growing- Gerascophobia or Gerontophobia.
Open spaces- Agoraphobia.
Open high places- Aeroacrophobia.
Operation, surgical- Tomophobia.
Opinions- Allodoxaphobia.
Opinions, expressing- Doxophobia.
Others, dependence on- Soteriophobia.
Otters- Lutraphobia.
Outer space- Spacephobia.

P -

Pain- Algiophobia, Ponophobia, Odynophobia or Odynephobia.
Paper- Papyrophobia.
Parasites- Parasitophobia.
Parents-in-law- Soceraphobia.
Peanut butter sticking to the roof of the mouth- Arachibutyrophobia.
Pellagra- Pellagrophobia.
Penis, erect- Medorthophobia.
Penis, esp erect- Phallophobia.
Penis, erect: seeing, thinking about or having- Ithyphallophobia.
Penis, losing an erection- Medomalacuphobia.
People- Anthropophobia.
People in general or society- Sociophobia.
People, deformed or bearing a deformed child- Teratophobia.
Philosophy- Philsosphobia.
Phobias- Phobophobia.
Phobic prefering fearful situations- Counterphobia.
Pins and needles- Belonephobia.
Pins- Enetophobia.
Place: locked in an enclosed place- Cleithrophobia, Cleisiophobia, or Clithrophobia.
Place, being in a dark or gloomy- Lygophobia.
Places, certain- Topophobia.
Places, crowded public- Agoraphobia.

Places, open high- Aeroacrophobia.
Places or things, narrow- Stenophobia.
Plants- Botanophobia.
Pleasure, feeling- Hedonophobia.
Poetry- Metrophobia.
Pointed objects- Aichmophobia.
Poison- Iophobia.
Poisoned, being- Toxiphobia, Toxophobia, or Toxicophobia.
Poliomyelitis, contracting- Poliosophobia.
Politicians- Politicophobia.
Pope- Papaphobia.
Poverty- Peniaphobia.
Praise, receiving- doxophobia.
Precipices- Cremnophobia.
Prescribing medicine for patients by a doctor- Opiophobia.
Priests or sacred things- Hierophobia.
Progress- Prosophobia.
Property- Orthophobia.
Prostitutes or venereal disease- Cypridophobia, Cypriphobia, Cyprianophobia, or Cyprinophobia.
Punishment or flogging- Mastigophobia.
Punishment by a rod or other instrument, or of being severely criticized- Rhabdophobia.
Punishment- Poinephobia.
Puppets- Pupaphobia.
Purple, color- Porphyrophobia.

R -

Rabies- Cynophobia, Hydrophobophobia, Hydrophobia, Kynophobia, or Lyssophobia.
Radiation or x-rays- Radiophobia.
Railroads or train travel- Siderodromophobia.
Rain- Ombrophobia or Pluviophobia.
Rape- Virginitiphobia.
Razors- Xyrophobia.
Rat, great mole- Zemmiphobia.

Rectum or rectal diseases- Proctophobia or Rectophobia.
Red color or blushing- Erythrophobia, Erytophobia or Ereuthophobia.
Relatives- Syngenesophobia.
Religion or gods- Theophobia.
Religious ceremonies- Teleophobia.
Reptiles- Herpetophobia.
Responsibility or duty, neglecting- Paralipophobia.
Responsibility- Hypengyophobia or Hypegiaphobia.
Ridiculed, being- Catagelophobia or Katagelophobia.
Riding in a car- Amaxophobia.
Right side, things on the right side of the body- Dextrophobia.
Rivers- Potamphobia or Potamophobia.
Road travel or travel- Hodophobia.
Robbers or being robbed- Harpaxophobia.
Rooms, empty- Cenophobia or Centophobia.
Rooms- Koinoniphobia.
Ruin- Atephobia.
Running water- Potamophobia.
Russians- Russophobia.

S -

Sacred things or priests- Hierophobia.
Satan- Satanophobia.
Scabies- Scabiophobia.
School, going to school- Didaskaleinophobia.
School- Scolionophobia.
Scientific terminology, complex- Hellenologophobia.
Scratches or being scratched- Amychophobia.
Sea or ocean- Thalassophobia.
Self, seeing oneself in a mirror- Eisoptrophobia.
Self, personal odor- Bromidrosiphobia or Bromidrophobia.
Self, being alone- Autophobia, Eremophobia, Eremiphobia or Isolophobia.
Self, being dirty- Automysophobia.
Self, being oneself- Autophobia.

Self, being seen or looked at- Scopophobia or Scoptophobia.
Self, being touched- Aphenphosmphobia.
Self, that one has a vile odor- Autodysomophobia.
Semen- Spermatophobia or Spermophobia.
Sermons- Homilophobia.
Sex- Genophobia.
Sex, opposite- Heterophobia or Sexophobia.
Sexual abuse- Agraphobia or Contreltophobia.
Sexual intercourse- Coitophobia.
Sexual love or sexual questions- Erotophobia.
Sexual perversion- Paraphobia.
Shadows- Sciophobia or Sciaphobia.
Sharks- Selachophobia.
Shellfish- Ostraconophobia.
Shock- Hormephobia.
Sin or of having committted an unpardonable sin- Enosiophobia or Enissophobia.
Sin- Hamartophobia.
Single: staying single- Anuptaphobia.
Sinning- Peccatophobia.
Sitting down- Kathisophobia.
Sitting- Cathisophobia or Thaasophobia.
Situations, certain- Topophobia.
Skin disease- Dermatosiophobia.
Skin lesions- Dermatophobia.
Skin of animals, fur- Doraphobia.
Sleep- Somniphobia.
Sleep or being hypnotized- Hypnophobia.
Slime- Blennophobia or Myxophobia.
Slopes, steep- Bathmophobia.
Small things- Microphobia, Mycrophobia.
Smells or odors- Olfactophobia.
Smothered, being or choking- Pnigophobia or Pnigerophobia.
Snakes- Ophidiophobia or Snakephobia.
Snow- Chionophobia.
Social (fear of being evaluated negatively in social situations)- Social Phobia.

Society or people in general- Anthropophobia or Sociophobia.
Solitude- Monophobia.
Sounds- Acousticophobia.
Sourness- Acerophobia.
Space, closed or locked in an enclosed space- Cleithrophobia, Cleisiophobia, Clithrophobia.
Space, outer- Spacephobia.
Spaces, confined- Claustrophobia.
Spaces, empty- Cenophobia, Centophobia or Kenophobia.
Spaces, open- Agoraphobia.
Speak, trying to- Glossophobia.
Speaking- Laliophobia or Lalophobia.
Speaking aloud, voices or noises, or telephones- Phonophobia.
Speaking in public- Glossophobia.
Specters or ghosts- Spectrophobia.
Speed- Tachophobia.
Spiders- Arachnephobia or Arachnophobia.
Spirits- Pneumatiphobia.
Stage fright- Topophobia.
Stairs or climbing stairs- Climacophobia.
Stairways- Bathmophobia.
Stand, inability to- Basiphobia or Basophobia.
Standing upright- Basistasiphobia or Basostasophobia.
Standing up- Stasiphobia.
Standing up and walking- Stasibasiphobia.
Stared at, being- Ophthalmophobia.
Stars- Siderophobia or Astrophobia.
Statements, false or myths or stories- Mythophobia.
Staying single- Anuptaphobia.
Stealing- Cleptophobia or Kleptophobia.
Step-father- Vitricophobia.
Steep slopes- Bathmophobia.
Step-mother- Novercaphobia.
Stings- Cnidophobia.
Stooping- Kyphophobia.
Stories or myths or false statements- Mythophobia.
Strangers or foreigners- Xenophobia.

Streets, crossing streets- Dromophobia.
Streets- Agyrophobia.
String- Linonophobia.
Storm, thunder- Brontophobia.
Stuttering- Psellismophobia.
Suffering and disease- Panthophobia.
Sun or sunlight- Heliophobia.
Sunshine or daylight- Phengophobia.
Surgeon's fear of operating: work or functioning- Ergasiophobia.
Surgical operations- Tomophobia.
Swallowing or eating- Phagophobia.
Symbolism- Symbolophobia.
Symmetry- Symmetrophobia.
Syphillis (lues)- Luiphobia or Syphilophobia.

T -

Tapeworms- Taeniophobia.
Taste- Geumaphobia or Geumophobia.
Technology- Technophobia.
Teenagers- Ephebiphobia.
Teeth- Odontophobia.
Telephones, noises or voices, or speaking aloud- Phonophobia.
Telephones- Telephonophobia.
Termites- Isopterophobia.
Tests, taking- Testophobia.
Tetanus or lockjaw- Tetanophobia.
Theaters- Theatrophobia.
Theology- Theologicophobia.
Things, many- Polyphobia.
Things, large- Megalophobia.
Things or places, narrow- Stenophobia.
Things, small- Microphobia or Mycrophobia.
Thinking- Phronemophobia.
Thunder- Ceraunophobia.
Thunder and lightning- Astraphobia, Astrapophobia, Brontophobia or Keraunophobia.

A List Of Phobias (Fear) From Wikipedia

Tickled by feathers or feathers- Pteronophobia.
Tied or bound up- Merinthophobia.
Time or clocks- Chronophobia.
Toads- Bufonophobia.
Tombstones- Placophobia.
Tornadoes and hurricanes- Lilapsophobia.
Touched, being touched- Aphenphosmphobia, Haphephobia or Haptephobia or Chiraptophobia.
Trains, railroads or train travel- Siderodromophobia.
Travel or road travel- Hodophobia.
Trees- Dendrophobia.
Trembling- Ttremophobia.
Trichinosis- Trichinophobia.
Tuberculosis- Phthisiophobia or Tuberculophobia.
Tyrants- Tyrannophobia.

U -

Ugliness- Cacophobia.
Undressing in front of someone- Dishabillophobia.
Urine or urinating- Urophobia.

V -

Vaccination- Vaccinophobia.
Vegetables- Lachanophobia.
Venereal disease or prostitutes- Cypridophobia, Cypriphobia, Cyprianophobia, or Cyprinophobia.
Ventriloquist's dummy- Automatonophobia.
Vertigo or dizziness when looking down- Illyngophobia.
Virginity, losing one's- Primeisodophobia.
Virgins or young girls- Parthenophobia.
Vision: double vision- Diplophobia.
Voices or noises, speaking aloud or telephones- Phonophobia.
Voids or empty spaces- Kenophobia.
Vomiting secondary to airsickness- Aeronausiphobia.
Vomiting- Emetophobia.

W -

Waits, long- Macrophobia.
Walking, standing up and- Stasibasiphobia.
Walking- Ambulophobia, Basistasiphobia or Basostasophobia.
Washing- Ablutophobia.
Wasps- Spheksophobia.
Water- Hydrophobia.
Waves or wave like motions- Cymophobia or Kymophobia.
Wax statues- Automatonophobia.
Weakness- Asthenophobia.
Wealth- Plutophobia.
Weapons, nuclear- Nucleomituphobia.
Weight, gaining- Obesophobia or Pocrescophobia.
Wet dreams- Oneirogmophobia.
Whirlpools or dizzyness- Dinophobia.
White, the color- Leukophobia.
Wild animals- Agrizoophobia.
Wind- Ancraophobia or Anemophobia.
Wine- Oenophobia.
Witches and Witchcraft- Wiccaphobia.
Women- Gynephobia or Gynophobia.
Women, beautiful- Caligynephobia or Venstraphobia.
Wooden objects or forests- Xylophobia.
Words- Logophobia or Verbophobia.
Words, long- Hippopotomonstrosesquipedaliophobia or Sesquipedalophobia.
Work or functioning; surgeon's fear of operating- Ergasiophobia.
Work- Ergophobia or Ponophobia.
Worms- Scoleciphobia.
Worms, being infested with- Helminthophobia.
Wrinkles, getting- Rhytiphobia.
Writing- Graphophobia.
Writing in public- Scriptophobia.

X -

X-rays or radiation- Radiophobia.

Y -

Yellow color- Xanthophobia.

Other books from the Author

The following is the list of other books the author has written which are available in Amazon and with the author; contact

Johnops51@yahoo.com
www.healingfacts.org

Escape from a Deserter's Death Penalty

An academic physician's candid personal testimony and his documentation of the various emotional sicknesses, which are dangerous to our lives and health, how to be prepared to deal with them.

Because his own death sentence was waived, he has waived the charges for the book. It is therefore yours free, for the asking. Visit our website to get more details.

Radiology for the Soul

202 nuggets in the pathway of our lives are presented in rhymes. Some are sharp stones and need to be avoided, some are like stable rocks in marshy areas of path to use as stepping stones. These are like traffic lights. We need to understand traffic rules and recognize the signs to reach our destination.
ISBN 0-9769249-3-5 $4.95

Crumbs under the Royal Table

A daily devotional of about three minutes a day, for people living in this frantic, hurried, time hungry, environment. This book will meet the need of the readers' hunger and thirst for life. Crumbs—they are not stale, but fresh and do not lack in nourishment.
ISBN 0-9769249-1-9 $9.95

A Tamil translation of this daily devotional is also available

The Lord's Prayer

Acknowledges the role of the Father, Son, and the Holy Spirit in the Lord's Prayer. It takes us into receiving kinship with God, responsibilities of citizenship, acknowledgment of the kingship of God, accepting the Lordship of the Son, restoring relationship with our neighbors, submission to discipleship through the Holy Spirit, our role in God's battle against evil, and our worship of the Triune God.
ISBN 1-59581-103-6 $6.75

War of our Cultures are Feeding the Vultures

A physician's candid look at the causes for our moral diseases in modern culture. Diseases flourish when there is lack of hygiene and these in turn result in an epidemic and kill millions around the globe. Lack of mental hygiene and deliberate toxic dumping on the public will destroy nations around the globe. The key for the clean-up is presented.
ISBN 1-594676-81-X $9.99

Deadly Snake Bite

Thousands die every year because of venomous snake bites on land and in water. Antivenin is the only possible help for those bitten. In

the spiritual realm, the venomous serpent has bitten all humans and the venom of sin will kill us, unless we get the antivenin administered to us in time. The Old Testament is the diagnostic component, pointing to "sin" as the venom killing us. The New Testament is the treatment part, offering to us the antivenin for sin, prepared by God through his own blood.
ISBN 0-9769249-0-0 $7.95

CPR from Above

It has now become a public priority to let every one learn how to help a person whose heart has stopped due to various causes. For all are becoming aware that if there is no oxygen (air supply) to the brain for three minutes, the brain may be damaged severely and if there is no oxygen to the brain for five minutes, the brain will die. As the heart pumps the blood containing oxygen in its red cells to the brain, the heart has to be manually pumped, and as oxygen has to be obtained from air, air has to be blown into the lungs while the heart is being mechanically pumped. Many have come back to life, after this procedure. These 5 minutes are crucial. If we give God even 5 minutes a day, he will revive and rejuvenate our hearts, lungs, and minds—not only for this world, but also for the next.
ISBN 1-59781-125-4 $17.00

ANGER Is Murder in the Mind

This book is meant to help young people deal with their anger in a positive way. It is richly illustrated by drawings of young people of different age groups. It addresses the common causes for anger, and the natural outcome of anger when it is not properly dealt with. In the present global age, not only adults, but even children in kindergarten are becoming victims of anger and violence. The educated adults do not know how to deal with it, as they themselves are victims of anger. This book offers a well-tested way to control anger.

The material in this book is not only for young people, but also for adults, pointing the way towards a less stressed out life.

ANGER - the Deadly Time Bomb in Our Hearts

Anger is like a tree with its numerous "bad roots." The roots feed, support, and hold the trunk, the tree, and its fruits above the ground for people to see. The tree of anger and its bad fruits are hazardous to human health. They cause many chronic and deadly diseases like heart attacks, paralyzing strokes, and breakdown of our immune system. The commonly used modern therapeutic systems have not been able to get any control on anger. A new look on a time-honored, well-documented treatment offered in a 2000 year old New Testament is presented as the only successful method of gaining control on anger. Mr. Gandhi and Rev. Martin Luther King adopted the principles in the New Testament, and were able to help mankind. A workbook on anger control is also incorporated, combining medical knowledge and principles that are to be applied.

Work Book for Stress, Tension, Anxiety,

Fear, Depression, and Anger
This book offers solution not only for anger, but also for other negative emotions like fears, anxiety, worry, tensions and stresses of different types. Satan the serpent has bitten humanity and has caused many sicknesses of body and mind. The venom has killed us spiritually.
Our mind is part of our soul, which Satan is trying to destroy. Jesus became human to give his blood as the only effective antidote for the serpent bite. The body has two major mechanisms to deal with all kinds of venom such as stress, angers, anxieties, depressions and tensions, operating through the autonomic nervous system and the endocrine system. One of them activates and the other calms us down to keep the balance or equilibrium. Otherwise, depressions,

psychotic changes and personality changes occur. The only proven antidotes are presented for us to peruse and to use.

If You LOVE to Live, Then Learn How to LOVE

The anatomy and physiology of terrestrial love and celestial love are evaluated as applicable in our day-today life. Love delights and takes us into still inadeqately explored ecstasies. Nevertheless, love can also hurt very deeply. Many people are afraid to take a step into the experience of love, fearing possible failure and hurt. Therefore, they miss the greatest experience they can enjoy in this life and the next. We have also touched upon the tip of the iceberg called celestial love.
ISBN 0-9769249-6-X $7.95

Triangle Illustrations, as Work Tool for Anger Control

A visual presentation of various causes for anger that makes us get upset. Biblical methods and illustrations are offered to enable God to "reset" us, and to make us grow spiritually. The format will also help teachers to educate and enable people of all ages to be benefited. The truth is that God is our head and we, all the people of different nations, color, caste, creed, language and religion are like different parts of one body. We need to be connected with God - our head - and with one another. The dangers of our disconnections to God and others are brought to the attention of the reader.

War or Peace

The world is torn because of escalating unrest, civil riots, and wars. All of us want peace but so far we have not achieved it. This little booklet offers the best answer and solution for healing of hurts and anger. If the content of this book is applied, we will find peace within ourselves, with one another in our homes, in our nations, and in our world. We will also find eternal peace with God our Father.

Cure for the Sick and Dying Homes (for adult reading)
ISBN 0-9769249-8-6

ANGER Is Murder in the Mind
ISBN 0-9769249-2-7

Work Book for Stress, Tension, Anxiety
ISBN 0-9769249-5-1

Triangle Illustrations, as Work Tool for Anger Control
ISBN 0-9769249-7-8

A physician's candid findings- that physical and moral hygiene are tightly integrated. Moral uncleanness causes many physical sickness and death. Home is where cleanliness matters most. This study is an analysis of thousands of homes and their problems; the solutions are Bible based. A useful book (illustrated) for those who want to get married, and those who are already married.

CPSIA information can be obtained at www.ICGtesting.com
Printed in the USA
LVOW012332140213

320170LV00002B/3/P